A2 Economics

KU-246-541

Contents

Introduction

■ ■ ■

Content Guidance

■ ■ ■

Questions and Answers

Data-response questions

Essay questions

Introduction

The aim of this guide is to prepare students for the AQA Unit 6 examination assessing A2 Module 6: Government Policy, the National and International Economy. You should use the guide as follows:

(1) Read the introduction.

(2) The second and third sections of the book should then be used as supplements to other resources, such as class notes, textbooks, *Economic Review* magazine and *AS/A-Level Economics Revision Notes*. (The last two of these are published by Philip Allan Updates.) Because it contains summaries rather than in-depth coverage of all the topics in the specification, you should not use the guide as your sole learning resource during the main part of the course. However, you may well decide to use the guide as the main resource in your revision programme. You are strongly advised to make full use of the Question and Answer section, especially in the revision period when you should be concentrating on improving your examination skills.

Examinable skills

The Unit 6 examination is $1\frac{1}{2}$ hours long, has a maximum mark of 100, and contains two sections, **Section A** and **Section B**, which each count for 50 marks. There is **one** compulsory data-response question (DRQ) in Section A, and **three** essay questions (EQs) in Section B, of which you should answer **one**. **There are no multiple-choice questions in any of the three A2 Unit examination papers**.

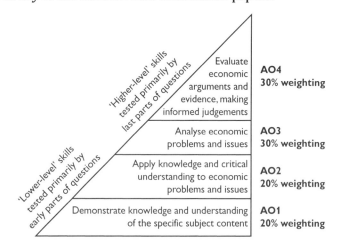

Figure 1 The examination's assessment objectives arranged along the incline of difficulty

The examination has four **assessment objectives** (AOs), which are shown in Figure 1, together with their examination weightings, arranged in an incline of difficulty. **Lower-level skills** of **knowledge** and **factual-recall** are shown in AO1 at the bottom of the incline. Moving up the incline, increasingly higher-level skills feature in the AOs:

application of knowledge and critical understanding (AO2); **analysis of problems** (AO3); and **evaluation of arguments and evidence** (AO4). Overall, 40% of the examination questions are knowledge-based, testing the lower-level skills in AOs 1 and 2. The remaining 60% of examination questions meet AOs 3 and 4. (In the AS examination, by contrast, 60% of the marks are awarded for lower-level skills and only 40% for higher-level skills. This means the A2 Unit examinations are more difficult than the AS Unit exams.)

Data-response skills

The **compulsory data-response question** in Section A contains **four** sub-questions, listed as (a), (b), (c) and (d). The mark allocation is as follows: **part (a): 4 marks; part (b): 6 marks; part (c): 10 marks; and part (d): 30 marks**. The Unit 6 examination data-response question contains more data than the AS data-response questions in the Units 1 and 2 examinations. The layout and structure of the question will be similar to the four data-response questions in the Question and Answer section of this guide. Each question is likely to contain two or three sets of data, usually extracted from different original sources, such as newspaper or magazine articles, or accessed from an internet website. The source will normally be indicated. With three data sets, the data will be labelled **Extract A, Extract B and Extract C**. One set of data is likely to be numerical: for example, a line graph, a bar graph, a pie graph or a table. The other data set(s) will be text.

An 'incline of difficulty' will be built into the DRQ, with the earlier parts of the question being the most straightforward. Typically, the key instruction words for each part of the DRQ will be:

(a) Describe (or possibly **Compare**)
(b) Explain
(c) Analyse
(d) Evaluate (or possibly **Assess**, or **Do you agree...?**, together with **Justify your argument**)

Because the module's title is Government Policy, the National and International Economy, the scenario of the DRQ may be an economy other than the UK: for example, the German, US or French economy. You should note that the national economy and the UK economy are not interchangeable terms. When an overseas country is used, the question will not require any detailed knowledge of the economy. The question will require the application of standard macroeconomic theory to explain, analyse and evaluate the information provided in the data. The question may also contain comparative data for a number of countries or groups of countries (e.g. EU or Eurozone countries, North America and Japan).

Parts (a) and (b) of the question will be marked using an **issue-based mark scheme** which lists the marks that can be awarded for the particular issues (and associated development) which might be included in the answer. Only lower-level skills (meeting AOs 1 and 2) are tested in parts (a) and (b) of the question.

As the key words indicate, parts (c) and (d) of the DRQ test the higher-level skills of **analysis** and **evaluation**. These parts of the question are marked using a **levels of response mark scheme**. The 'levels' mark scheme for part (c) of the DRQ has only **three levels, the content of which varies in every examination**.

Part (d) of the DRQ differs from the earlier parts (especially parts (a) and (b)) in three significant ways. First, and most obviously, the last part of the question carries many more marks than the earlier three parts — 60% of the total marks for the question and 30% of the total marks for the whole paper. If you time the examination incorrectly and fail to develop your answer to part (d) beyond a cursory footnote, you will reduce considerably your chance of achieving grade A. Second, whereas parts (a) and (b) should be answered briefly, you are expected to write an extended answer of at least a page for part (d). Think of this as a 'mini' essay. (Part (c), which carries 10 marks, falls between these extremes. Its answer requires some development, but not as much as part (d).) Third, 'higher-level' skills of **analysis** and particularly **evaluation** are expected for part (d).

A levels of response mark scheme containing **five levels** is used for part (d) of the DRQ and for part (b) of all the essay questions in Section B. You must familiarise yourself with the 'levels' mark scheme and bear it in mind when you practise the last part of data-response questions and essay questions.

The key command word to **evaluate** or **assess** must be obeyed for your answer to reach the higher Level 4 and Level 5 standards of attainment set out in the levels mark scheme. Part (d) of the DRQ in Section A and part (b) of the essay questions in Section B are virtually the only parts of the whole examination paper set specifically to meet AO4: evaluation of arguments and evidence, and the making of informed judgements. (1 mark out of 10 in part (c) of the DRQ is also awarded for evaluation.) Your answer must evaluate the different arguments you set out. With many questions, discussion should centre on evaluating the advantages and disadvantages of (or the 'case for' versus the 'case against', or the costs and benefits of) a course of action mentioned in the question.

Finally, always try to finish your answer with a conclusion, the nature of which should vary according to the type of discussion or evaluation required. The conclusion might judge the relative strengths of the arguments discussed, possibly highlighting the most important argument. With many questions it is more appropriate to conclude whether, on balance, the 'case for' is stronger than the 'case against' and to provide some credible and reasoned justification for your opinion.

Essay question skills

Whereas the DRQ in Section A of the Unit 6 examination is compulsory, you must select **one essay question from a choice of three** when answering Section B of the paper. Choice of question is obviously very important. Because the module's title is Government Policy, the National and International Economy, you should expect one of the three essay questions to be on the international economy.

As is the case with parts (a) and (b) of the data-response question, part (a) of the essay question tests the lower-level skills and assessment objectives of knowledge and understanding, and application. The advice already given on how to answer part (d) of the compulsory data-response question is equally applicable to answering part (b) of your chosen essay question.

The synoptic requirement of the Unit 6 examination

The Unit 6 and Unit 5 examinations at A-level are **synoptic**. To understand this, compare the Unit 6 examination with the Unit 2 AS examination on the National Economy. Questions in the Unit 2 examination only test knowledge and understanding of terms and concepts set out in the AQA Module 2 specification. For example, the Unit 2 examination cannot contain a question on a macroeconomic topic which requires you to apply a microeconomic concept (for example, market failure) to explain why the government intervenes in the national economy.

Such a question could, however, appear in the Unit 6 examination. It is also important to distinguish between vertical synopticity and horizontal synopticity. **Horizontal synopticity** requires the application of a Module 5 microeconomic concept or theory to answer a Unit 6 macroeconomic question. By contrast, **vertical synopticity** requires the use of AS macroeconomic concepts and theories (in the Module 2 specification) to answer Unit 6 macroeconomic questions.

Checklist of relevant AS Unit 2 terms and concepts

- the meaning of national income and output, and its measurement: GDP
- understanding data in the form of index numbers and other forms of data presentation
- the distinction between nominal and real economic variables
- the objectives of a government's macroeconomic policy: full employment, growth, controlling inflation, a satisfactory balance of payments
- booms, recessions, trend growth and actual growth, output gaps
- the main causes (types) of unemployment
- excess demand and rising costs as causes of inflation
- the role of monetary policy (interest rates) in controlling inflation
- the meaning of aggregate demand and aggregate supply
- using the AD/AS macroeconomic model to analyse events taking place in the economy, the level of economic activity and the effect of government intervention and policy
- components of aggregate demand and their effect on economic activity: consumption, investment, government spending and exports
- leakages or withdrawals of demand from the economy: saving, taxation and imports
- fiscal policy used both as a demand-side policy to manage aggregate demand and as a supply-side policy to improve the efficiency and competitiveness of markets and to shift the LRAS curve rightwards

- supply-side policies to make labour and goods markets function more efficiently and competitively
- the current account of the balance of payments
- the effect of the exchange rate on the economy

A suggested strategy for tackling the examination

(1) On opening the examination booklet, turn to Section B and spend a minute or so reading all three essay questions before making a preliminary choice of a favoured question. For each question, look carefully at part (b), which is the part for which higher-level analysis and evaluation marks are awarded. Beware of choosing a question with an apparently straightforward part (a), but a part (b) that you do not fully understand.

(2) Then go back to Section A, glance through the questions at the end of the data and spend about 3 minutes reading the extracts containing the data.

(3) Assuming you have 40 minutes to answer the data-response question, write the following time allocations in the margin against each part of the question: part (a) 3 minutes; part (b) 5 minutes; part (c) 8 minutes; part (d) 24 minutes.

(4) Answer all the parts of the question, preferably in the correct order, sticking rigidly to the time allocation. Do not over-develop your answers to parts (a) and (b) of the question, but remember that a single sentence seldom answers the question properly. Remember also that many candidates fail to do themselves justice in the exam because they overwrite their answers to parts (a) and (b), and do not leave enough time to answer part (d) properly.

(5) Label each of your answers with the correct letter: (a), (b), (c), (d). Nothing annoys an examiner more than a script in which all the answers are jumbled together.

(6) Do not waste time copying out the questions, but leave a few lines at the end of each part of your answer in case you have time at the end of the exam to add an extra sentence or two.

(7) For each part of the question, think very carefully about what it requires you to do, and make sure you **obey** the key instruction word.

(8) You will probably not have time to write plans for each part of the question, except for part (d), where a short plan might help you to write a better answer.

(9) Having completed your answer to the compulsory data-response question in Section A, turn to Section B, and read the questions carefully again. Choose the question that you think you can answer best, taking into account the difficulty of *both* parts of the question.

(10) Assuming you have 45 minutes to answer your chosen question, write the following time allocations in the margin against each part of the question:

part (a) 18 minutes; part (b) 27 minutes. This time allocation, which uses up all the available time, can be shortened slightly to allow yourself up to 5 minutes to read through all your answers at the end.

(11) If you believe it will help you, write a short plan for part (a). Then write your answer to part (a), making sure you define all the terms and concepts that you apply — both those in the wording of the question and those you introduce from your own knowledge. You need to display the skills of **knowledge and understanding**, **application**, and perhaps some **analysis**, to stand a chance of gaining full marks for part (a) of the essay question.

(12) Having completed your answer to part (a) within 18 minutes, write a plan for part (b). If appropriate, list the 'case for' and the 'case against' arguments that you intend to develop in your answer and list any theories you are going to use to analyse the issue(s) posed by the question.

(13) Start your answer to part (b) by stating how you are interpreting the question, and by indicating briefly the arguments to be developed in the main body of your answer. Then develop each argument, making sure you use appropriate theory and analysis. You can also pick up evaluation marks if you indicate, as you go along, how significant each argument is. But make sure you write a concluding paragraph, several lines long, devoted to an overview of the arguments and containing an overall conclusion. This is where the examiner finds it easiest to award evaluation marks.

(The advice given in points (12) and (13) above is equally applicable for answering part (d) of the compulsory data-response question in Section A of the examination.)

Revision planning

The revision strategy below is based on the use of this guide, supplemented by other resources such as the notes you have built up over your course of study and favoured textbooks. The programme is designed for the 3-week period before the examination. The strategy assumes you are revising at least two other A-level subjects (and for one or both of the Units 4 and 5 examinations) during the same period, but are able to devote a session of 2 hours (plus half an hour for short breaks) to Unit 6 every other day, with shorter follow-up sessions on the intervening days. You should revise solidly for 6 days a week, but allow yourself one day off a week to recharge your batteries. The strategy can be modified to meet your personal needs and preferences: for example, by shortening each revision session and/or extending the sessions over a revision period longer than 3 weeks.

(1) Revise one topic from the Content Guidance section of this guide per revision session. Divide each revision session into four half-hour periods during which you are working solidly and without distraction, interspersed with 10-minute breaks.

(2) Proceed through the topics in the order they appear in the guide:
Week 1: Topics 1–3
Week 2: Topics 4–6
Week 3: Topics 7–9

(3) Vary the activities you undertake in each 30-minute period of a revision session. For example, spend the first 30 minutes reading through the Essential Information section of the topic. List key terms and concepts on a piece of paper. After a short break, use the second 30-minute period to check more fully the meaning of the key terms and concepts in your class notes and/or an economics textbook. Then after a second short break, check which essay questions and parts of data-response questions in the Question and Answer section of the guide test aspects of the topic you are revising. Spend the rest of the 30 minutes answering some or all of the questions. In the final 30-minute period — or perhaps in a follow-up session a day or two later — read through any candidate answers that relate to the parts of the essay question or DRQ covered by the topic, before reading the examiner's comments on the question(s).

To vary your revision programme, and to make sure you reinforce and retain the vital information revised in the longer sessions, you should fit some of the activities suggested below into follow-up sessions. Activities suitable for follow-up and 10-minute sessions include the following:

- **Write definitions** of some of the key terms and concepts relating to the topic revised on the previous day. Check each of your definitions against the correct definition in this guide, or in a textbook or your class notes.
- **Draw key diagrams** relating to the topic. Check any diagram you draw against a correct version of the diagram, making absolutely sure that the diagram is labelled correctly and clearly.
- Whenever you make mistakes, **repeat these exercises** every day or so, until you have eliminated all the mistakes.
- **Answer questions** from past AQA examination papers and from AQA's *Specimen Units and Mark Schemes* booklet, which your teacher should have. Ask your teacher for all the relevant June and January AQA past exam papers that are available at the time you take the examination. Identify and answer questions from past papers, which relate to the topic just revised. Then check your answer(s) against the AQA mark scheme(s) to see how you could improve your answer(s).

Note: If you wish to buy your own copies of past examination papers and mark schemes, contact: The Publications Department, The Assessment and Qualifications Alliance, Aldon House, 39 Heald Grove, Manchester M14 4NA (tel: 0161 953 1170).

Content
Guidance

In contrast to AS Module 2: The National Economy, which is concerned with elementary macroeconomics, Module 6: Government Policy, the National and International Economy, centres for the most part on more **advanced** macroeconomics. As the specification states, Module 6 builds on the knowledge and skills learnt in Module 2. It requires candidates to use and evaluate more complex macroeconomic models than those introduced in Module 2, and to develop further their critical approach to economic models and methods of enquiry. Nevertheless, you should be aware that, as in Module 2, the **aggregate demand/aggregate supply (AD/AS) macroeconomic model** is the most important of all the models you need to know. You should also realise that the AD/AS model is unlikely to be mentioned in the wording of a question. Along with **circular flow diagrams** and **production possibility frontiers**, AD/AS is an essential part of the theoretical tool kit needed when analysing and evaluating the problems, puzzles or issues posed by a question. You should also note that more understanding of the derivation of the AD/AS model is required in the Unit 6 examination than in the Unit 2 examination.

Phillips curve analysis, both in the short run and the long run, is also required for answering Unit 6 examination questions. This is a completely new part of the specification which does not figure in Module 2, except in the narrow sense of awareness of a conflict between macroeconomic objectives.

Unlike in Module 2, and as the module title indicates, **international economics** is an important part of Module 6. As previously noted, you should expect at least one question on international economics in the Unit 6 examination. The main international topics you are expected to know are trade theory, the case for import controls, the balance of payments, exchange rates and globalisation.

The introduction to this section of the guide (pp. 13–14) contains a summary of the AQA specification for Module 6: Government Policy, the National and International Economy. This is followed by more detail about each section of the specification under the following headings:

- The growth of modern macroeconomics (pp. 15–18)
- Economic growth, the business cycle and living standards (pp. 19–23)
- Aggregate demand and aggregate supply (pp. 23–27)
- Unemployment and inflation (pp. 28–33)
- The Phillips curve and the natural rate of unemployment (pp. 33–38)
- Monetary policy (pp. 38–43)
- Fiscal policy, taxation and public expenditure (pp. 43–48)
- International trade and globalisation (pp. 48–53)
- The balance of payments, exchange rates and EMU (pp. 53–59)

Introduction to the specification

The AQA specification for Unit 6 contains the following sections.

15.1 Growth of the economy and cyclical instability

Module 2 introduced candidates to the economy's **actual growth rate** and its **trend growth rate**, and to the fluctuations around the trend rate of growth associated with the **business cycle**. At A-level you must be able to apply at least two **theoretical explanations of the business cycle**, although the specification is not prescriptive of what the explanations should be, apart from noting how **supply-side or demand-side shocks** can trigger cyclical fluctuations. Detailed theories of economic growth are *not* required.

You are expected to interpret different types of national income data, possibly for a range of countries, but you do not need to know technical details of national income accounts. It is necessary to understand the **costs and benefits of economic growth**, and the **use and limitations of national income as an indicator of changes in living standards**. You must be able to discuss the **impact of growth on individuals and the environment**. Knowledge of the **sustainability of growth** is needed, which implies an understanding of **resource depletion and degradation**.

15.2 Inflation and unemployment

This section of the specification builds on the knowledge acquired in Unit 2 on the **types or causes of unemployment** and **demand-side (demand-pull)** and **supply-side (cost-push) causes of inflation**. Both unemployment and inflation need to be analysed in the **AD/AS theoretical framework**. AD/AS needs to be understood in greater detail than in Unit 2, particularly with reference to the **natural rate of unemployment** and **Phillips curve analysis**. As with AD/AS, you must understand the difference between **short-run and long-run Phillips curves**. Neither **consumption** nor **investment** is mentioned in the Unit 6 specification, but along with the **national income multiplier**, they may be tested synoptically.

Along with other explanations of inflation, you must know the **quantity theory of money** as a special case of demand-pull inflation. The specification states that candidates should understand and evaluate the **monetarist model of inflation**, which implies some knowledge of the role of **expectations** in the inflationary process. You must also know how **index numbers** are calculated and used to **measure inflation**, and the **effects of inflation on individuals and the performance of the economy**.

15.3 Managing the national economy

The Module 6 specification requires knowledge and understanding of **monetary policy**, **fiscal policy** and **supply-side policy** as three of the main ways of managing the national economy. You need to study all these in greater detail and with more rigour than for AS.

You must also appreciate the **exchange rate as a target and instrument of fiscal policy**, and the **interrelationships between fiscal and monetary policy**. You should understand the relationship between interest rates and the exchange rate and how the exchange rate influences policy objectives, such as inflation, unemployment and the balance of payments. Knowledge of the **conflicts between policy objectives** is also more sophisticated at A-level than at AS.

Particular knowledge of the role of the **Monetary Policy Committee of the Bank of England** is required, especially in the context of its history of hitting or failing to hit the **inflation rate target** set by the Treasury. Detailed knowledge of financial markets is *not* needed, but you do need to understand that **bank deposits**, which are the main component of the money supply, are liabilities of the private enterprise banking system. Since it is unable to control bank deposits directly, the Bank of England attempts to influence monetary conditions via the effect of **interest rate changes** on the general public's desire to hold bank deposits. Detailed knowledge of the **money supply** is no longer required.

15.4 The international economy

The international economy is covered in much greater depth in the Module 6 specification than in the Module 2 specification. Module 6 requires knowledge of the **benefits of international trade** and the **principle of comparative advantage**, together with the possible **costs of international specialisation**.

Globalisation, developing countries and the **European Union** all figure to a lesser or greater extent in this part of the specification. **Globalisation** should be given special attention via its effects, for good and for bad, on trade and the **location decisions of multinational or transnational corporations**. **Development economics** is mentioned in terms of the nature and importance for both parties of trade between developed and developing countries. **Theories of protectionism** must be put into a European context related to the European Union as a **customs union**. Candidates, especially those preparing for coursework rather than for the European Union case study in A-level Module 4, must also remember that knowledge of **the advantages and disadvantages of the European Monetary Union (EMU)** and the **single European currency** is also required.

Coverage of trade theory must include **patterns of trade** between the UK and the rest of the world. Some knowledge of the **capital account of the balance of payments** is also needed, but not in technical detail. However, the nature and significance of both **short-term and long-term international capital flows** should be understood. You must revise the current account of the balance of payments learnt for the AS course, and **link current account deficits and surpluses to the exchange rate**. Knowledge of both freely floating and fixed exchange rates is required, together with their links to interest rates and monetary policy and to domestic macroeconomic policy and conflicts.

The growth of modern macroeconomics

These notes, which relate to AQA specification sections 15.1, 15.2 and 15.3, prepare you to answer AQA examination questions on:
- the approach of Keynesian and free-market economists to how the economy works
- the changing views of economists regarding the major objectives of macro-economic policy

Essential information

The Keynesian Revolution

These notes provide an overview of how macroeconomics has changed in recent economic history. More than any other individual, **John Maynard Keynes** created modern macroeconomics. Until **monetarism** in the 1970s, macroeconomics and **Keynesian economics** were much the same thing, growing out of Keynes's great and influential book, *The General Theory of Employment, Interest and Money*, published in 1936. Before Keynes, most economists belonged to the **neo-classical** or **pre-Keynesian school** (or what is now called the **free-market school**). Pre-Keynesian economists believed that **market forces operating in competitive markets provide a self-adjusting mechanism**, which, in the long run, automatically ensures full employment and economic growth.

Figure 1 illustrates the **pre-Keynesian explanation of employment and unemployment**, in which full employment is determined at the level of employment where the aggregate demand for labour equals the aggregate supply of labour, at the wage W_{FE}. According to this theory, **classical** or **real-wage unemployment** is caused by wage rates being too high, at W_1 rather than W_{FE}.

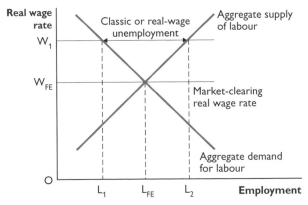

Figure 1 The pre-Keynesian theory of unemployment

Pre-Keynesians believed that real-wage unemployment is temporary. Market forces would cure the problem by bidding down wages until the number of workers willing to work equals the number that firms wish to hire. But in the 1930s, the market mechanism failed to cure unemployment. If an individual employer, or all the firms in a particular industry, cut wages in a single labour market within the economy, more workers are hired. Aggregate demand for output is not affected if the firm or industry is only a tiny part of the whole economy. But at the macro level, if real wages are cut throughout the economy, aggregate demand falls and firms cannot sell their output. Wage cuts may therefore increase rather than reduce unemployment.

Keynes argued that **deficient aggregate demand** causes unemployment. The **paradox of thrift** explains this. **Saving**, regarded as a **virtue** at the individual level, becomes a **vice** at the aggregate level if people save too much and spend too little. The policy solution is to inject demand back into the economy to counter the leakage of demand through saving. In its **fiscal policy**, the government should run a **budget deficit** (i.e. set G > T). In essence, the government borrows the excess savings of the private sector, which it spends itself, thereby injecting demand back into the economy and preventing the emergence of deficient demand.

The Keynesian era

The **Keynesian era** began shortly after 1945 when governments started to use demand management policies to achieve the objective of full employment. The era ended in the 1970s with the advent of monetarism and the free-market or new-classical revival. In the intervening 30 years governments in many industrial countries, including the United Kingdom, used **fiscal policy** to manage aggregate demand. When unemployment was high, the government expanded demand by increasing the budget deficit. As full employment was approached, increased demand caused imports to rise and the current account of the balance of payments to deteriorate. It also triggered **demand-pull inflation** since, in the short run at least, output could not rise to meet the increase in demand. A contractionary or deflationary policy of increased taxation and public spending cuts would be implemented. Macroeconomic policy in the Keynesian era was dominated by **'stop–go'** — successive periods of **deflation** and **reflation** resulting from the management of aggregate demand.

The crisis in Keynesian economics

For much of the Keynesian era, the policy of **fine-tuning** aggregate demand to a level consistent with full employment, but without excessive inflation, appeared to be working, and economic growth was more or less continuous. But at the same time, inflation began to creep up. Opponents of Keynesianism became more confident in their criticism of Keynesian theories and policies, arguing that Keynesian demand management could achieve full employment only through injecting greater and greater doses of inflation into the economy. Once achieved, full employment was becoming less and less sustainable.

By the mid-1970s Keynesianism was in disarray. Keynesian theory had been relatively invulnerable to serious attack as long as Keynesian economic management performed reasonably well when measured against the **main objectives of economic policy: full employment, growth, control of inflation and a satisfactory balance of payments**. Keynesianism became vulnerable to attack when a simultaneous failure to achieve any of the primary policy objectives occurred in the mid-1970s. The **stagflation** or **slumpflation** of stagnant or declining output and growing unemployment combined with accelerating inflation, together with social conflict over the distribution of income and a deteriorating balance of payments, signalled the end of the Keynesian era.

The monetarist or free-market counter-revolution

The 1970s witnessed the **decline of Keynesianism** and the **ascendancy of monetarism**. Monetarists believe that the immediate cause of all inflation lies in a prior increase, permitted by governments, of the money supply.

Monetarism began in 1956 when Professor Milton Friedman revived the old pre-Keynesian theory of inflation, the **quantity theory of money**. The quantity theory argues that the **quantity of money in the economy determines the price level** and the rate of inflation. If the government allows the money supply to expand at a rate faster than the growth of output, the price level rises when people spend the excess money balances they hold.

Monetarist policies were implemented in the UK in the late 1970s and the early 1980s. The government abandoned **discretionary demand management policies** and based policy on **automatic policy rules**. The **monetary policy rule** centred on the publication of a **target rate of growth of the money supply** for a medium-term period of about 3 years ahead, accompanied by the announcement that monetary policy would be implemented to 'hit' the money supply target. Other aspects of macro policy, including **full employment** as the **major policy objective**, were subordinated to the monetary policy aim of controlling monetary growth in order to achieve the new prime policy objective of **controlling inflation**. The government also adopted a **fiscal policy rule** based on **reducing the size of public sector spending** and **borrowing** as proportions of national output. Fiscal policy became subordinated to the needs of monetary policy, a situation that still generally exists today.

The decline of monetarism and the growth of supply-side economics

Monetarism never really worked, with the growth in the money supply often outstripping the growth in prices. This unfortunate fact cast great doubt on the central assumption of narrow monetarism, namely that an increase in money supply causes inflation. But although the strictly 'monetarist' aspects of macroeconomic policy were quietly dropped after the mid-1980s, later UK governments have remained committed to the 'wider' free-market aspects of economic policy adopted during the monetarist era. In particular, **supply-side economics** came to the fore, which aimed to improve the economy's supply side and its ability to produce.

Recent developments in macroeconomic policy

As noted, **demand management policies** were abandoned in the monetarist era and replaced with **automatic policy rules**. However, the **breakdown of monetarism** eventually led to a **return to demand management**, but with a significant difference from its previous Keynesian use.

In the late 1980s and early 1990s, it was realised that demand must be managed to prevent the recessionary phase of the business cycle from becoming too depressed and the boom stage from becoming overheated and too frothy. For the most part, however, **fiscal policy is no longer used to manage aggregate demand**, although the government's budget functions as an **automatic stabiliser**, moving into deficit or surplus to help stabilise the business cycle. As explained later (see p. 45), fiscal policy is now bound much more by automatic rules (the **golden rule of borrowing** and the **sustainable investment rule**).

Monetary policy is now used to control the level of spending in the economy. In May 1997, the Bank of England was made operationally independent of the government and given the task of 'hitting' the inflation rate target set by the government of 2.5% a year. Monetary policy has therefore replaced fiscal policy as the main tool of demand management, with fiscal policy being used primarily to create the conditions deemed necessary to promote macroeconomic stability.

Examination questions and skills

AQA economics examinations *do not* test knowledge of events longer ago than about 10 years before the examination. Nevertheless, it is a good idea to possess such knowledge, if only to make better sense of current and very recent policies, and events in the UK and world economies. These notes, which provide this information, should be treated as a precursor to the more detailed and up-to-date information in the topics that follow. A good understanding of how macroeconomic theories and policies have developed over the years will improve the quality of your answers to DRQ2 and EQs 1, 2 and 3 in this book.

Common examination errors

- Failing to understand the major objectives of macroeconomic policy, and the ways in which their relative importance has changed.
- Confusing policy objectives and policy instruments.
- Treating Keynesianism and fiscal policy as interchangeable terms.
- Treating monetarism and monetary policy as interchangeable terms.
- Failing to appreciate the difference between discretionary economic policy and automatic policy rules.

Economic growth, the business cycle and living standards

These notes, which relate to AQA specification section 15.1, prepare you to answer AQA examination questions on:
- economic growth and the business cycle
- the costs and benefits of economic growth
- national income and standards of living

Essential information

What you already know about economic growth and the business cycle

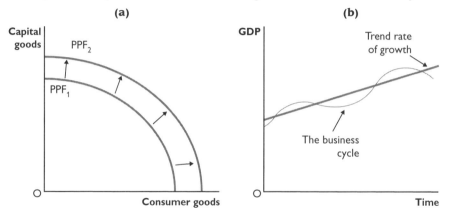

(a)   (b)

Figure 2 Aspects of economic growth

In your AS course, you learnt that **economic growth** can be defined as an **increase in the economy's production potential**. In panel (a) of Figure 1 this is illustrated by the outward movement of the **economy's production possibility frontier** from PPF$_1$ to PPF$_2$. (A rightward movement of the economy's **long-run aggregate supply (LRAS) curve** also illustrates economic growth.) By contrast, a movement from a point *inside* the frontier to a point on the frontier is called **economic recovery**, though some economists call this *short-term* economic growth. Panel (b) shows the economy's **trend rate of growth**, together with its **actual growth path** depicted by the **boom** and **recession** of the **business cycle**. A recession occurs when **real output** falls for 6 months or more. The economy's **output gap**, which measures the difference between the *actual* level of real output and the output that *would* be produced if the economy grew continuously at its trend rate, is another term you learnt at AS.

Economic growth

Economic growth results from **investment** in new **capital goods** (**physical capital**), which enlarges the **national capital stock**, and in human beings (**human capital**). But while investment is an important factor in the growth process, it may not be as important as **technical progress**. Until quite recently, economists had little to say about the causes of technical progress, treating it as 'manna from heaven'. However, an important new theory, known as **endogenous growth theory**, incorporates the causes of technical progress into the theoretical explanation of the growth process. The theory suggests that governments can create supply-side conditions that favour investment and technical progress. These conditions include **external economies** for businesses, often in the form of **infrastructure**, and a **judicial system** which protects **patents** and other **intellectual property rights**, and which enforces the **law of contract**.

Fluctuations in economic activity

Fluctuations in economic activity occur in three main ways: the **business cycle**, **seasonal fluctuations** and a possible **long cycle** that lasts perhaps 60 years. Business cycles, which are 4–12 years long, are caused primarily by **fluctuations in aggregate demand** (i.e. by leftward and rightward shifts in the AD curve). There are a number of different theories of the business cycle and it is advisable to learn at least two theories in some depth. Examples include the following:

- Rapid growth produces a **speculative bubble** in asset prices (e.g. housing and/or shares), which rise far above the assets' real value. The bubble bursts, destroying **consumer and/or business confidence**. People stop spending and the economy falls into recession.
- The **political business cycle**. UK governments, which are elected every 4 or 5 years, may try to engineer a **pre-election boom** (to buy votes) and then deflate or contract the economy immediately after the election — until the next pre-election boom.
- Random **demand shocks** (and sometimes **supply shocks**) hit and throw the economy off course. (See DRQ1 for an explanation of outside shocks hitting the economy.)

Seasonal fluctuations are related to climate: for example, very cold winters closing down the building trade. At the opposite extreme, **long cycles of about 60 years** have been identified. Significant **improvements in technical progress** (on the supply-side of the economy) cause firms to invest in completely new technology, which triggers a long period of boom. Electrification and the automobile have had this effect. At present, information and communication technology (ICT) may be having a similar effect, possibly creating a **new economy**. In the past, long booms have run out of steam when the innovating technology becomes fully used — until, of course, the next burst of technical activity creates another boom.

Stabilising the business cycle

Demand management policies can be used to try to reduce fluctuations in the business cycle. In the Keynesian era, fiscal policy was used in this way, but these days monetary policy is used to do this. In a boom when the economy is overheating, the Bank of England raises interest rates to **contract** or **deflate** aggregate demand. By contrast, in a recession the Bank of England cuts interest rates to **reflate** or boost aggregate demand. But successful stabilisation requires accurate timing. Bad timing can destabilise the business cycle and make it more volatile. And by causing long-term risky investments to be abandoned in favour of less risky short-term projects, unexpected interest rate (or tax) changes may affect competitiveness and long-term growth adversely.

The costs and benefits of economic growth

The **ultimate purpose of economic activity is to improve economic welfare** and people's **standards of living**. Economic growth can help to achieve this, but only if growth is compatible with **economic development**. Economic growth, which is *measured by* (though not *defined by*) the annual percentage growth in real national output, can have a number of costs that reduce economic welfare or happiness.

By contrast, economic development, which includes the **quality** and not just the **quantity** of growth, is measured by:

- a **general improvement in living standards** that reduces poverty and human suffering
- **greater access to resources**, such as food and housing, required for basic human needs
- **greater access to opportunities for human development**, e.g. through education and training
- **environmental sustainability and regeneration**, through reduced resource **depletion** and **degradation**

Resource depletion occurs when finite resources such as oil are used up, and when soil fertility or fish stocks decline irreversibly. By contrast, **resource degradation** is best illustrated by pollution of air, water and land. To benefit people in the long run, growth (and development) must be sustainable. **Sustainable economic growth** means the use of:

- renewable rather than non-renewable resources
- technologies that minimise pollution and other forms of resource degradation

The use and limitations of national income as an indicator of changes in living standards

When using national income figures to measure economic welfare, **real national income per capita** should be used to overcome the fact that prices rise and population changes. Used in this way, national income figures provide quite a good estimate of the first two elements in the standard of living shown below:

standard of living =	economic welfare derived from goods and services purchased in the market economy	+	economic welfare derived from public goods and merit goods provided collectively by the state	+	economic welfare derived from quality of life factors, external benefits minus external costs or intangibles

However, national income statistics both under-estimate and over-estimate economic welfare and living standards for the whole population. They *under-estimate* activity because the **non-monetised economy** (such as housework and DIY) is under-represented, and because activity undertaken illegally in the **'hidden' economy** is omitted. The value of **positive externalities** shown in the third element of standards of living is also omitted from national income statistics. **Improvements in the quality of goods** may also be under-represented in national income statistics.

An important reason why national income statistics *over-estimate* living standards and welfare relates to **negative externalities** such as pollution and congestion, and to activities such as crime. What is in effect a welfare loss may be shown as an increase in national output, falsely indicating an apparent welfare gain. For example, the stresses and strains of producing an ever-higher national output lead to a loss of leisure time and make people ill more often. Loss of leisure and poorer health are welfare losses. But in the national accounts, these show up as extra production and as extra consumption of healthcare, both of which imply a welfare gain. Likewise, installing **'regrettables'** such as burglar alarms raises national income, but most people would prefer a crime-free environment and no burglar alarms. Significant **disparity in income distribution** also reduces the value of national income statistics as a measure of welfare. In developing countries the **income distribution** is typically extremely unequal and only a small fraction of the population may benefit materially from economic growth.

Comparing national income between countries

Comparisons of national income per head between countries are misleading if the relative importance of the non-monetised economy is significantly different. There are also differences in the degree of statistical sophistication in data collection, particularly between developed and developing countries, and a lack of international uniformity in methods of classifying and categorising national accounts. Further problems occur when making comparisons if different commodities are consumed. For example, expenditure on fuel, clothing and building materials is likely to be greater in developed countries with cold climates than in much warmer developing economies. But we must take care not to deduce from this single fact that greater expenditure — for example, on home heating — indicates higher real income and living standards.

A common method of comparing GNP per capita in different countries is to convert the GNP figures for each country into a common currency such as the US dollar. However, this calculation suffers from the assumption that the exchange rates between local currencies and the dollar are valued correctly, in the sense that a dollar's worth of output in one country becomes immediately and accurately comparable with a dollar's worth of output in any other country. This can never be so. Exchange rate changes only reflect the price changes of internationally traded goods. As there is a much wider gap in developing countries than in developed countries between the price changes of internationally traded and non-traded goods, GNP figures measured in US dollars tend to underestimate real levels of income and output in developing economies. The solution to this problem is to establish **purchasing power parity (PPP) exchange rates**, which means that a PPP dollar, or any PPP currency, buys the same quantity of a good everywhere in the world.

content guidance

Examination questions and skills

Part (a) of DRQ1 asks for a comparison of rates of economic growth in a number of developed countries including the UK. The other parts of the question require explanation, analysis and evaluation of some of the conditions that affect economic growth and performance. Part (b) of EQ1 asks whether a government committed to the free market should reduce the role of fiscal policy in promoting economic growth. Part (a) of EQ2 asks for an evaluation of the various factors that might increase economic growth, while part (b) centres on national income as a measure of economic welfare.

Examination questions which require detailed explanation of theories of growth are *not* likely to be set. You might, however, be asked to explain the causes of the business cycle, possibly disguised in a question on the causes of fluctuations in economic activity.

Common examination errors

- Measuring economic growth in terms of the growth of **nominal output** rather than **real output**.
- Confusing economic growth with economic recovery.
- Confusing a cyclical upturn with the trend rate of economic growth.
- Failing to understand the difference between economic growth and economic development.
- Failing to understand sustainable economic growth, resource depletion and resource degradation.

Aggregate demand and aggregate supply

These notes, which relate to AQA specification section 15.2, prepare you to answer AQA examination questions on:
- understanding the nature of aggregate demand and aggregate supply
- applying the AD/AS model to analyse and evaluate problems and policy

Essential information

What you already know about aggregate demand and aggregate supply
The **aggregate demand/aggregate supply (AD/AS) macroeconomic model**, which is illustrated in Figure 3, is just as important in Module 6 as it is in Module 2. You do not need to learn much more about AD/AS for the Unit 6 exam, but you are required to *apply* the model to explain, analyse and evaluate macroeconomic problems and policy in greater depth than for your AS course.

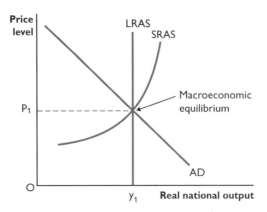

Figure 3 The AD/AS macroeconomic model

As in the AS course, the AD/AS macroeconomic model provides the theoretical framework that you are expected to use to analyse and evaluate economic problems and policy relating to **economic growth**, **inflation** and **unemployment**.

The **aggregate demand (AD) curve** in Figure 3 shows the **total quantities of** *real* **output** that all economic agents — households, firms, the government and the overseas sector — **plan to purchase** at different domestic price levels, when everything other than the price level is held constant. If any of the components of aggregate demand change, the curve will shift rightward or leftward, depending on the nature of the change. For example, an **increase in consumer or business confidence** shifts the AD curve rightward, via the effect on consumption or investment. **Expansionary monetary and fiscal policy** have a similar effect. By contrast, **contractionary policy** or **a collapse in consumer or business confidence** causes the AD curve to shift leftward.

You learnt in your AS course that there are two **aggregate supply (AS) curves**, an upward-sloping **short-run aggregate supply (SRAS) curve** and a vertical **long-run aggregate supply (LRAS) curve**. However, you did not learn much about *why* AD and AS curves have the shapes illustrated in Figure 3. The shapes of the curves, particularly the difference between the **SRAS** and the **LRAS curves**, are explained in the next section.

The aggregate demand (AD) curve

Two factors explain the *slope* **of the AD curve**, as distinct from a *shift* **of the curve**. The first is a **wealth** or **real balance effect**. Assuming a given *nominal* stock of money (or money supply) in the economy, a decrease in the price level increases people's *real* money balances, i.e. the same amount of money will now buy more. An increase in real money balances makes people feel wealthier, and since consumption is positively related to wealth, aggregate demand rises as the price level falls. The second effect follows from this. When the supply of any commodity (in this case, real money balances) increases relative to demand, its price falls. The rate of interest is the price of money; hence an increase in real money balances causes the rate of interest to fall, further stimulating consumption and investment spending.

Short-run aggregate supply

Just as the AD curve shows the total quantities of real output that economic agents plan to purchase at different price levels, so the **AS curve** shows the quantities of real output that businesses plan to produce and sell at different price levels. There are a number of possible shapes for the short-run AS (SRAS) curve. These different shapes carry different implications for macroeconomic policy.

Panel (a) in Figure 4 shows the **inverted L-shaped AS curve**, based on the **Keynesian view of how the economy works**, which was prevalent a generation ago. During the Keynesian era, it was widely believed that expansionary fiscal or monetary policy, which shifts the aggregate demand function from AD_1 to AD_2, **reflates** real output, which increases from y_1 to y_2, with the price level remaining unchanged at P_1.

The Keynesian view was that firms respond to increased demand by increasing output, without requiring an increase in the price level to persuade them to increase output or supply. But when full employment is reached, at real output level y_{FE}, a further increase in aggregate demand (for example, to AD_3) causes prices and not output to rise. Excess demand pulls up the price level to P_2 in a **demand-pull inflation**.

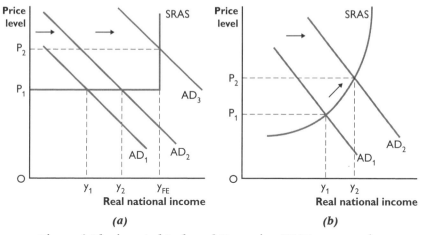

Figure 4 The inverted L-shaped Keynesian SRAS curve and an
upward-sloping SRAS curve

Economists now generally reject the inverted L-shaped AS curve, believing instead that, in the short run at least, the AS curve slopes upwards as depicted in panel (b) of Figure 4. The upward-sloping SRAS curve stems from two important elements of microeconomic theory: the assumption that **firms aim to maximise profit**; and the **law of diminishing returns** or **diminishing marginal productivity**. Following an expansion of aggregate demand from AD_1 to AD_2 in panel (b), which disturbs an initial macroeconomic equilibrium, the price level must rise to create conditions in which profit-maximising firms are willing to supply more output. To produce more output, more workers must be hired, but as they are hired, their marginal productivity falls and the marginal cost of production rises. When marginal costs rise, the prices charged by firms must also rise, otherwise it is not profitable to produce the extra output. The result is the upward-sloping short-run AS curve, which shows that a higher price level is required for firms to supply more output.

The vertical long-run aggregate supply (LRAS) curve

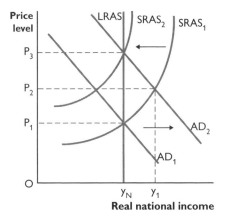

Figure 5 The vertical LRAS curve

A rise in the price level needed to increase SRAS causes the **real wage** paid to workers to fall — providing money wage rates remain unchanged. What happens next depends on how workers respond to a real wage rate cut. There are two possibilities. If workers refuse to supply the extra labour needed to produce the extra output, income or output falls back to the equilibrium level of real output (y_N in Figure 5) prevailing before the rightward shift of the AD curve. But if workers respond to the higher price level by pushing up money wage rates to restore their real wage rates, then the short-run AS curve will shift leftward from $SRAS_1$ to $SRAS_2$ because costs of production have risen. As a result, the 'new' AD and AS curves (AD_2 and $SRAS_2$) once again intersect at the original equilibrium level of output y_N. For free-market economists, y_N is the **natural level of output** towards which market forces and a flexible price mechanism eventually adjust. It is the **long-run equilibrium level of output** associated with the **natural levels of employment and unemployment** of labour. The vertical line drawn in Figure 5 at the natural or equilibrium level of output is the **long-run aggregate supply (LRAS) curve**. The LRAS curve carries the message that the short-run expansionary effect on output and employment, resulting from the government increasing aggregate demand beyond the economy's natural ability to produce additional output, is negated in the long run by the way the supply side of the economy responds to the demand stimulus.

The AD/AS model and economic policy

The AD/AS model is particularly useful for analysing the effect of an increase in aggregate demand on the economy because it addresses the important issue of whether **expansionary fiscal policy and/or monetary policy** will increase real output and jobs (i.e. will it be **reflationary**), or whether the price level will increase instead (i.e. will it be **inflationary**). In the short run, as we have seen, the answer to this key macroeconomic question depends on the **shape of the SRAS curve**, but in the long run, the vertical slope of the LRAS curve means that expanding aggregate demand to a level beyond y_n increases the price level but not real output.

The LRAS curve is located at the natural or equilibrium level of real output, which is the level of output consistent with the **natural rate of unemployment** in the labour market. Because output and employment are assumed to be at their natural or equilibrium levels, free-market economists conclude that it is generally irresponsible for governments to use expansionary fiscal or monetary policy to try to increase national output and employment. While such policies may succeed in the short run, though at the expense of inflation, they are doomed eventually to fail. In the long run, output and employment fall back to their equilibrium or natural levels, which are determined by the economy's production potential or ability to supply. Thus, instead of expanding demand to reduce unemployment **below** its natural rate, free-market economists believe that the government should use microeconomic supply-side policies *to reduce the natural rate itself.*

But if the economy is initially producing *below* y_n, there is a role for increasing aggregate demand to create the demand needed to absorb the economy's ability to supply more goods. However, as noted, increasing aggregate demand *beyond* y_n raises prices rather than output.

Examination questions and skills

It is worth repeating that the aggregate demand/aggregate supply (AD/AS) macro-economic model is unlikely to be mentioned in a Unit 6 examination question, but that, as in the AS course, the model provides the main theoretical framework that you are expected to apply when analysing and evaluating macroeconomic problems and government policies. The AD/AS model can be used to explain economic growth, employment and unemployment, inflation, and both demand-side and supply-side economic policy.

DRQ2 on inflation and deflation is especially appropriate for AD/AS analysis, as are EQ1 on monetary and fiscal policy, and EQ3 on inflation.

Common examination errors

- Confusing macroeconomic AD and AS curves with microeconomic demand and supply analysis.
- Labelling the vertical axis of an AD/AS diagram as *inflation* rather than the price *level*.
- Confusing AD/AS diagrams with Phillips curve diagrams.
- Wasting time deriving AD or AS curves, instead of applying them to analyse the issue posed by the question.
- Failing to relate AD/AS diagrams to demand-side and supply-side economic policy.
- Failing to see the link between the natural level of real output in an AD/AS diagram and the natural rate of unemployment in a Phillips curve diagram.

Unemployment and inflation

These notes, which relate to AQA specification section 15.2, prepare you to answer AQA examination questions on the causes and consequences of:

- unemployment
- inflation

Essential information

What you already know about unemployment and inflation

When studying AS Module 2: The National Economy, you learnt that full employment and unemployment can be illustrated on a **production possibility frontier (PPF) diagram**, and that there are **two main causes of inflation**: **demand inflation** and **cost inflation** (respectively known also as **demand-pull** and **cost-push inflation**). In panel (a) of Figure 6, full employment occurs at all points on the economy's PPF, such as A and B. By contrast, the distance from a point inside the frontier such as C to the frontier represents unemployment. In panel (b), a rightward shift of aggregate demand pulls up the price level (demand inflation). Panel (b) also illustrates cost-push inflation caused by a leftward shift of aggregate supply.

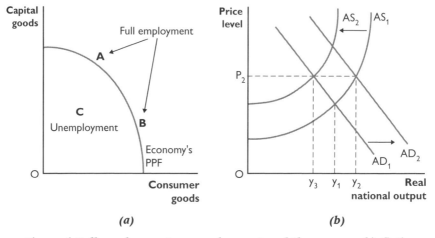

(a)   *(b)*

Figure 6 Full employment, unemployment and the causes of inflation

Who are the unemployed?

There are many people in the UK who are of working age and not working, but who are not 'officially' unemployed. These 'inactive' people of working age include people who stay at home, students without a part-time job and those who retire early. The government publishes two measures of unemployment, the **claimant count** and the **International Labour Organisation (ILO)** measure, based on the **Labour Force Survey**. In the early 2000s, the claimant count, which measures those who are unemployed and actually claiming benefit in the form of **jobseeker's allowance**, fell below

1 million, but the ILO measure, which includes the unemployed not claiming benefit, is about half a million higher.

The causes of unemployment

Before Keynes, the **classical or real wage theory of unemployment** (explained on p. 15) was the dominant theory of unemployment. Other types or causes of unemployment are **frictional**, **structural** and **demand-deficient**.

Frictional and structural unemployment

In a dynamic economy, change takes place constantly, with some industries declining and others growing. As new products are developed and demand and cost conditions change, firms demand more of some labour skills while the demand for other types of labour declines. Economists use the terms **frictional** and **structural unemployment** to describe the resulting unemployment. **Frictional unemployment**, as its name suggests, results from frictions in the labour market that create a delay or time-lag during which a worker is unemployed when moving from one job to another. Because there will always be some frictional unemployment, even when there is 'full employment', frictional unemployment is also called **equilibrium unemployment**. Some frictional unemployment can be explained by the **search theory of unemployment**. Suppose that a worker earning £600 a week in a skilled occupation loses her job. There are plenty of vacancies for unskilled workers, at much lower wage rates, but none at £600. In this situation, the worker chooses to remain voluntarily frictionally unemployed, partly because the wage and working conditions do not meet her aspirations, and partly because better-paid vacancies exist which she does not, as yet, know about, but which may be discovered through actively searching the labour market.

Structural unemployment results from the **structural decline** of industries unable to compete or adapt in the face of either changing demand and new products, or changing ways of producing existing products and the emergence of more efficient competitors in other countries. The growth of international competition has been a particularly important cause of structural unemployment. **Technological unemployment** is a special case of structural unemployment resulting from the successful growth of new industries using labour-saving technology such as automation.

Keynesian or demand-deficient unemployment

Keynes believed that **deficient aggregate demand** was a major cause of persistent mass unemployment. One of the main disputes separating Keynesian and free-market economists centres on the nature of demand-deficient unemployment. Economists generally agree that **temporary unemployment** (called **cyclical unemployment**) may be caused by a lack of demand in the **downswing of the business cycle**. However, Keynes went further, arguing that the economy could settle into an **under-full employment equilibrium** caused by a continuing lack of effective aggregate demand. As the sections on **monetary policy** and **fiscal policy** explain (pp. 38–43, 43–48), Keynesian economists believe that governments should actively manage the level of aggregate demand to reduce or eliminate demand-deficient unemployment.

The consequences of unemployment

Unemployment represents a **waste of human capital**. Nevertheless, free-market economists believe that a certain amount of unemployment is necessary to make the economy function better. By providing downward pressure on wage rates, unemployment may reduce inflationary pressures. However, it tends to widen income differentials and increase absolute and relative poverty. Higher unemployment means greater spending on unemployment and poverty-related benefits, the opportunity cost of which is less spending on the provision of hospitals, schools and other useful resources.

Governments generally implement policies to try to reduce unemployment, but the appropriate policy obviously depends on identifying the underlying cause of unemployment correctly. For example, if unemployment is diagnosed in terms of demand deficiency, when the 'true' cause is structural, a policy of fiscal or monetary expansion to stimulate aggregate demand will be ineffective and inappropriate. Indeed, **reflation of demand** in such circumstances would probably create excess demand, which would raise the price level in a **demand-pull inflation**, with no lasting beneficial effects on employment.

It is now widely agreed, by Keynesians as well as by free-market economists, that **the cause of long-term unemployment in countries such as the UK lies on the supply side of the economy** rather than on the demand side. There is much disagreement, however, on the appropriate policies to improve supply-side performance. Free-market economists argue that poor supply-side performance is the legacy of decades of Keynesian interventionism a generation ago. To cut frictional, structural and real-wage unemployment, the economic role of the state must be reduced rather than extended. By setting markets free, encouraging competition and fostering private enterprise and the entrepreneurial spirit, an enterprise culture can be created in which the price mechanism, and not the government, will deliver economic growth and reduce unemployment. In the free-market view, the correct role of government is to create the conditions, through controlling inflation, promoting competitive markets and maintaining the rule of law and social order, in which the market mechanism and private enterprise can function properly. Some Keynesians disagree, arguing that unemployment results from a massive market failure, which can only be cured by interventionist policies to modify the market and make it function better.

The causes of inflation: demand-pull and cost-push inflation

Inflation is defined as a persistent or **continuous rise in the price level**, or as a **fall in the value of money.** Demand-pull inflation is caused by **excess demand** in the economy pulling up the price level. The **quantity theory of money** (which is at the heart of **monetarist** economic theory) is the oldest theory of demand-pull inflation. According to the quantity theory, the government creates or condones an expansion of the money supply greater than the increase in real national output. As a result, households and firms hold excess money balances which, when spent, pull up the price level — given the fact that real output cannot expand in line with the increase in spending power.

The quantity theory of money can be developed from the **equation of exchange**:

money supply $\times$ velocity of $=$ price level $\times$ total transactions
(or stock of circulation in the economy
money) of money

or: MV = PT

For an **increase in the money supply** (on the left-hand side of the equation) to **pull up the price level** (on the right-hand side), the **velocity of circulation of money** (how often money is spent) and **total transactions** (an indicator of **real national income**) must both be constant, or at least stable. **Keynesians** do not accept these **monetarist assumptions**. As a result, the quantity theory of money and the causes of inflation form a major area of dispute between Keynesian and free-market economists.

Because governments allow the money supply to expand excessively, according to the quantity theory, they are blamed for inflation. **Keynesian theories of demand-pull inflation** generally ignore the money supply and locate the cause of inflation in the factors that increase consumer spending and borrowing, and in the tendency of governments to **increase public spending and budget deficits** (in **fiscal policy**) in order to win elections.

Many Keynesians favour the **cost-push theory** of inflation, which can be illustrated by a **leftward shift in the short-run AS curve**. Cost-push theory locates the cause of inflation in **trade union activity** and in other causes of **market imperfection** in both the product market and the labour market. In labour markets, their strength enables trade unions to bargain for money wage increases in excess of any rise in labour productivity. Monopoly firms pay these wage increases, partly because of the costs of disrupting production, and partly because they believe that they can pass on the increasing costs as price rises. Cost-push theories usually assume that wages are determined through the process of **collective bargaining**, while in the goods market, prices are formed by a **'cost-plus' pricing rule** through which monopolistic firms add a standard profit margin to their costs when setting prices. Thus **trade union militancy** or **'pushfulness'** and **big business's monopoly power** are blamed for inflation.

The consequences of inflation

Everybody agrees that inflation can have serious adverse effects or costs. However, the seriousness of the adverse effects depends on whether inflation is **anticipated** or **unanticipated**. If inflation could be anticipated with complete certainty, it would pose few problems. Households and firms would simply build the expected rate of inflation into their economic decisions, which would not be distorted by wrong guesses. When inflation is relatively low, with little variation from year to year, it is relatively easy to anticipate next year's inflation rate. Creeping inflation can be associated with growing markets, healthy profits and a general climate of business optimism, **greasing the wheels of the economy**. Indeed, a low rate of inflation may be a necessary cost of expansionary policies to reduce unemployment. But some free-market economists argue that inflation acts like **sand in the wheels of the economy**, making it less efficient and competitive. If the sand-in-the-wheels effect is stronger than the greasing-the-wheels effect, the costs or disadvantages of inflation exceed the benefits or advantages.

Particular consequences of inflation are as follows:

- **Distributional effects**. Weaker social groups in society on fixed incomes lose, while those in strong bargaining positions gain. Also, with rapid inflation, **real rates of interest may be negative**. In this situation, lenders are really paying borrowers for the doubtful privilege of lending to them, and inflation acts as a hidden tax, redistributing income and wealth from lenders to borrowers.
- **Distortion of normal economic behaviour**. Inflation can distort consumer behaviour by causing households to bring forward purchases and hoard if they expect the rate of inflation to accelerate. Similarly, firms may divert funds out of productive investment in fixed investment projects into unproductive commodity hoarding and speculation.
- **Breakdown in the functions of money**. In a severe inflation, money becomes less useful and efficient as a **medium of exchange** and **store of value**. Rapidly changing prices also erode money's functions as a **unit of account** and **standard of deferred payment**. In a hyperinflation, less efficient **barter** replaces money and imposes extra costs on most transactions.
- **International uncompetitiveness**. When inflation is higher than in competitor countries, exports increase in price, putting pressure on a **fixed exchange rate**. With a **floating exchange rate**, the exchange rate falls to restore competitiveness, but rising import prices may fuel a further bout of inflation.
- **Shoe leather and menu costs**. Consumers incur *shoe leather costs*, spending time and effort shopping around and checking which prices have or have not risen. By contrast, *menu costs* are incurred by firms, having to adjust price lists more often.

Examination questions and skills

Examination questions are likely to cover the causes of unemployment and inflation, interrelationships between the two (see the next section), and application of AD/AS theory to explain the causes of both, the costs and benefits of inflation, and how economic policy might reduce unemployment or inflation.

In recent years, the fear of **deflation** (continuously *falling* prices) has to some extent replaced the fear of inflation and continuously *rising* prices. You must read DRQ2, and the candidate's answer and examiner's comments on this question, to build up an understanding of the problems that deflation might bring.

Common examination errors

- Assuming that full employment means that everybody is employed.
- Failing to understand the difference between and the adequacy of the two ways of measuring unemployment.

- Confusing frictional and structural unemployment.
- Writing about relatively trivial causes of unemployment, such as seasonal and casual unemployment, when the question is about the more important frictional, structural and demand-deficient causes.
- Confusing inflation with a one-off price change, or with relative price changes.
- Failing to appreciate conflicts between full employment and price stability as macroeconomic policy objectives (see the next topic).
- Assuming that inflation is always bad and never good, and that deflation must be good because inflation is bad.
- Failing to understand how price indices such as the RPI measure inflation.

The Phillips curve and the natural rate of unemployment

These notes, which relate to AQA specification section 15.2, prepare you to answer AQA examination questions on:
- the short-run and the long-run Phillips curve
- factors determining the natural rate of unemployment (NRU)
- the implications of the Phillips curve and the NRU for economic policy

Essential information

What you already know about the Phillips curve and the natural rate of unemployment

At AS, you learned about the conflict between full employment and controlling inflation, as macroeconomic policy objectives. However, the Module 2 specification makes no mention of the Phillips curve or of the natural rate of unemployment.

The original (short-run) Phillips curve

At the height of the Keynesian era two generations ago, **A. W. Phillips** argued that a stable inverse statistical relationship exists between the rate of **wage inflation** and the percentage of the labour force unemployed. (More usually these days, the Phillips curve measures the inverse relationship between **unemployment and the rate of** *price* **inflation**.)

The **Phillips curve** is *not* a theory of inflation, but it gives support to both the main theories of inflation. In the **demand-pull theory**, falling unemployment is associated with excess demand, which pulls up wages and prices. In the **cost-push theory**, falling unemployment increases trade union power, enabling unions to use their monopoly power to push for higher wages.

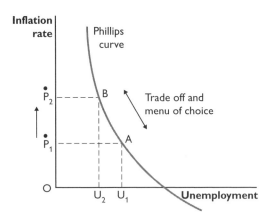

Figure 7 The short-run Phillips curve

Although the Phillips curve illustrates the **conflict between full employment and control of inflation** as policy objectives, it also suggests how the conflict can be dealt with. Suppose unemployment is initially U_1 and the rate of inflation is $\dot{P}_1$, with the economy at point A on the Phillips curve. By expanding aggregate demand, the government can move the economy to point B. Unemployment falls to U_2, but at the cost of a higher rate of inflation at $\dot{P}_2$.

The breakdown of the Phillips relationship

The Phillips curve indicates that by using **demand management policies**, governments can **trade off** between the number of jobs in the economy and the rate of inflation. Points such as A and B on the Phillips curve represent a **menu of choice** from which governments can choose when deciding an acceptable combination of unemployment and inflation. But in the 1970s, accelerating inflation and growing unemployment occurred together. The breakdown of the Phillips curve relationship was a major cause of the free-market counter-revolution that replaced Keynesianism.

The long-run Phillips curve (LRPC) and the natural rate of unemployment (NRU)

Economists now generally recognise that the Phillips curve in Figure 7 is a **short-run Phillips curve (SRPC)**, representing the *short-run* relationship between inflation and unemployment. In Figure 8(a), a **vertical long-run Phillips curve (LRPC)** has been added to the diagram, cutting the short-run Phillips curve where the rate of inflation is zero. The rate of unemployment at this point is called the **natural rate of unemployment (NRU)**, depicted by the symbol U_N.

Free-market economists believe that it is impossible to reduce unemployment below the NRU, except at the cost of suffering an ever-accelerating inflation, which, by eventually accelerating into a **hyperinflation**, eventually destroys the economy. They argue that the original, Keynesian, explanation of the (short-run) Phillips curve wrongly took into account only the *current* rate of inflation, and ignored the important influence of the *expected* rate of inflation. Figure 8(b) shows what happens when the role of expectations is brought into the Phillips curve diagram.

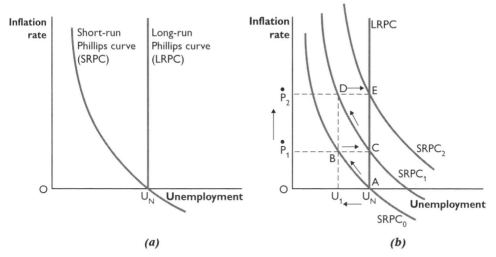

Figure 8 The long-run Phillips curve and the natural rate of unemployment

We shall assume that the rate of growth of labour productivity is zero and that the rate of *price* inflation equals the rate of *wage* inflation. The economy is initially at point A, with unemployment at the natural rate U_N. At point A, the rate of inflation is zero, as is the rate of increase of money wages. We shall also assume that people form their expectations of *future* inflation in the next time period solely on the basis of the *current* rate of inflation. At point A, current inflation is zero, so workers expect the future rate of inflation also to be zero.

Suppose the government expands demand, to trade off along Phillips curve $SRPC_0$ to a point such as B, where unemployment at U_1 is below the natural rate, U_N. Inflation initially rises to $\dot{P}_1$ or 5%. But a point such as B is unsustainable. This is because, for workers to supply more labour, the **real wage** must rise, yet a rising real wage causes employers to demand less labour. In the short run, more workers may indeed enter the labour market in the **false belief** that a 5% increase in *money* wages is also a *real* wage increase. This is called **money illusion**. Similarly, firms may be willing to employ more labour if they also suffer money illusion, believing falsely that rising prices mean that sales revenues are rising faster than labour costs.

To sustain an increase in employment *above* the natural rate (and to reduce unemployment *below* the NRU), **workers and employers must suffer permanent money illusion in equal but opposite quantities** to keep expectations of inflation, formed in the previous time period, consistently below the actual rate to which inflation has risen. But workers continuously adjust their expectations of future inflation to the rising actual rate and bargain for ever-higher money wages to restore the real wage to the level necessary to reduce unemployment below U_N. As they do this, the short-run Phillips curve shifts outward from $SRPC_0$ to $SRPC_1$ and so on. There is a **separate short-run Phillips curve for each expected rate of inflation**. *Further out* short-run Phillips curves such as $SRPC_1$ and $SRPC_2$ are associated with higher expected rates of future inflation. Conversely, the short-run Phillips curve shifts inwards when the expected rate of inflation falls.

Free-market economists argue that, in the long run, the only way to keep unemployment *below* the NRU is to permit the money supply to expand and finance an ever-accelerating inflation. For this to happen, inflation has to accelerate above the rate that workers and firms are expecting: for example, from $\dot{P}_1$ to $\dot{P}_2$. But, as noted earlier, an accelerating inflation will eventually create a hyperinflation, which, in the resulting breakdown of economic activity, will almost certainly increase the NRU. Any attempt to reduce unemployment below the NRU is therefore foolhardy and irresponsible. In the short run it accelerates inflation, while in the long run it perversely increases the NRU to an unnecessarily high level.

If the government realises that it made a mistake initially when expanding the economy to point B, it can stabilise the rate of inflation at 5%. Workers and employers see through their earlier money illusion and realise that they have **confused money quantities with real quantities**. They refuse respectively to supply, and to demand, the labour necessary to keep unemployment below the NRU. The economy then moves to point C in Figure 8 (b). Once point C is reached, any further expansion of aggregate demand would move the economy to point D and an inflation rate of $\dot{P}_2$ — and to a repeat of the process just described, but starting from a higher initial rate of inflation.

Adaptive expectations versus rational expectations

The theory just described is based on the **theory of adaptive expectations**, in which workers and firms form expectations of what will happen in the *future* only on the basis of what is happening *currently* and upon what has happened in the *recent* past. However, **new-classical economists** favour an alternative theory of how expectations are formed, called the **theory of rational expectations**. According to this theory, it is unrealistic to assume that workers and firms, acting rationally in their self-interest, form expectations of future inflation *solely* on the basis of current or recent inflation. If they can forecast the results of events taking place in the economy now, self-interest dictates that they should quickly modify their economic behaviour to take account of the most up-to-date information available. New-classical economists reject the idea that economic agents suffer money illusion for quite long periods — a vital component in the explanation of the short-run Phillips curve. If expectations are formed *rationally* rather than *adaptively*, any attempt by a government to reduce unemployment below its natural rate by expanding demand fails, leading solely to accelerating inflation. The correct way to reduce unemployment is to **reduce the natural level itself**, rather than to **expand demand to try to reduce unemployment below the NRU**. To do this, the government should use appropriate **free-market supply-side policies**.

Supply-side policy and the natural rate of unemployment

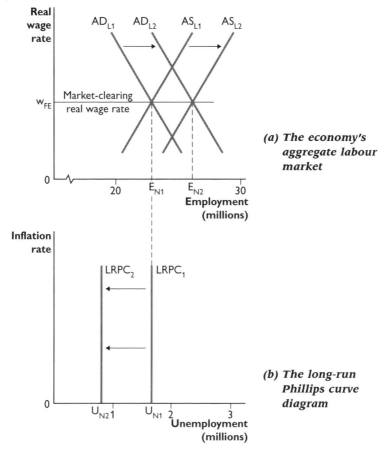

(a) The economy's aggregate labour market

(b) The long-run Phillips curve diagram

Figure 9 Supply-side policies increasing the natural level of employment and reducing the natural level of unemployment

Figure 9 shows how **supply-side policy**, in the form of business and income tax cuts, can shift the long-run Phillips curve leftwards and reduce the NRU. A business tax cut reduces costs of production, thereby shifting the **aggregate demand curve for labour** (shown in panel (a)) from AD_{L1} to AD_{L2}. Likewise, income tax cuts granted to workers shift the **aggregate supply curve of labour** from AS_{L1} to AS_{L2}. As a result, the **natural level of employment** in the **aggregate labour market** increases from E_{N1} to E_{N2}. This in turn reduces **frictional unemployment** (and the NRU) in panel (b) of the diagram, shifting the long-run Phillips curve leftwards from $LRPC_1$ to $LRPC_2$. The NRU thus falls from U_{N1} to U_{N2}.

Examination questions and skills

Whereas an AS question is likely to ask about the *causes* of unemployment and inflation, an A2 question is more likely to test understanding of the *conflicts* and *trade-*

offs between full employment and control of inflation. Questions might mention the Phillips curve, but they are likely to leave it to you to distinguish between the short-run and long-run Phillips curves and to apply them as analytical tools. Likewise, the natural rate of unemployment is a key analytical concept that may or may not be mentioned in a question. It is important to use the NRU when explaining and evaluating the significance of both demand-side and supply-side economic policies.

DRQ2 tests knowledge and understanding of causes of inflation, and its opposite, deflation. The Phillips curve is not mentioned explicitly in this question, but a good answer might make use of the Phillips curve and the natural rate of unemployment.

Common examination errors

- Confusing short-run and long-run Phillips curves.
- Confusing Phillips curve diagrams with AD/AS diagrams.
- Confusing a reduction of unemployment *below* the NRU with a *leftward shift* of the NRU.
- Failing to relate the NRU to the analysis of supply-side economic policy.
- Failing to relate NRU analysis to the functioning of the aggregate labour market.

Monetary policy

These notes, which relate to AQA specification sections 15.2 and 15.3, prepare you to answer AQA examination questions on:
- the instruments and objectives of monetary policy
- the role of the Bank of England in implementing monetary policy in the UK
- the link between financial markets and monetary policy

Essential information

What you already know about monetary policy

In your AS course, you learnt that **monetary policy** attempts to achieve the **policy objectives** set by the government using **monetary instruments** such as **interest rates** and **controls on bank lending**. You also learned that the **Bank of England**, the country's **central bank**, raises or lowers interest rates, and that this shifts the AD curve leftwards or rightwards in the AD/AS macroeconomic model, thereby affecting output, employment and the rate of inflation.

Money and monetary policy

Money is best defined by the two main functions it performs in the economy, as a **medium of exchange** (or **means of payment**) and as a **store of value** or **wealth**. **Cash** and **bank deposits** are the two main forms of money. When implementing monetary policy, the Bank of England controls the supply of cash to the banking system. However, the Bank of England always issues enough cash to enable the commercial banks to meet customer demand for cash, thereby maintaining confidence in the banking system. The fact that the Bank of England acts as **lender of last resort** to the banking system gives the Bank its main monetary policy instrument: the **rate of interest** at which the Bank of England lends cash to the banking system. Cash is really just the *small change of the monetary system*. **Bank deposits**, which are liabilities of the private enterprise banking system, are by far the major part of modern money. For the most part, monetary policy centres on the Bank of England raising or lowering its interest rate to control or influence the ability of the commercial banks to create deposits when they lend to customers.

Monetarism

For a fairly short period from the late 1970s until the mid-1980s, UK monetary policy was **monetarist**. Monetarists are so called because they believe that inflation is caused by prior excess growth of the **money supply**, via the **quantity theory of money**. They also believe, first, that control of inflation should be the government's main policy objective and, second, that to control inflation the **rate of growth of the money supply must be strictly controlled**. But in the short-lived monetarist experiment, monetarist policies did not work, and UK monetary policy ceased to be monetarist after the mid-1980s. However, two important features of monetarist monetary policy have survived: first, monetarists disliked unnecessary government intervention in the economy and therefore **abandoned the controls on bank lending** used by the Keynesians and, second, **control of inflation** has continued through the 1990s and early 2000s to be the **ultimate objective** of UK monetary policy.

The framework of UK monetary policy

The framework of current UK monetary policy was created by a Conservative government in 1992, modified by the incoming new Labour government in 1997, and given a few minor changes when the decision was made not to join the euro (at least for the time being) in 2003. Before 1997, the **Chancellor of the Exchequer** (in charge of the **Treasury**) and the **Governor of the Bank of England** (who were the **monetary authorities**) implemented monetary policy. The authorities raised or lowered interest rates to try to keep the inflation rate below a target rate set by the government. The policy had a **deflationary bias**, since the further inflation fell below the target rate, the greater the deemed success of monetary policy.

In 1997, the Labour government reformed the monetary policy framework, primarily by **making the Bank of England operationally independent** in implementing policy to 'hit' the inflation rate target set by the government, and by **establishing the Monetary Policy Committee (MPC)** to formulate and implement policy to achieve this goal. The Labour government's monetary policy should be regarded as a reform of the policy inherited from the Conservatives, rather than as a root-and-branch upheaval. The following features, which pre-date May 1997, continue as essential elements of the current policy:

- Monetary policy is implemented to 'hit' an inflation rate target set by the government. The policy instrument used to achieve this is the Bank of England's 'official' interest rate — a change in which affects other short-term interest rates.

This is partly through an 'announcement' effect, and partly through the Bank of England's intervention in financial markets, which massages other short-term interest rates in the direction of the official rate.

- The inflation rate target is now symmetrical. Prior to May 1997, monetary policy aimed to get the inflation rate on or below the target rate set by the government and the policy probably had an in-built deflationary bias. Arguably, this is no longer the case. The MPC is now prepared to reduce interest rates to stimulate output and employment if it believes that, on unchanged policies, an inflation rate below the target rate will be accompanied by an undesirable fall in output and employment. In the government's words: 'the primary objective of monetary policy is price stability. But subject to that, the Bank of England must also support the government's economic policy objectives, including those for growth and employment.'

- The money supply and the exchange rate are now used as 'indicators' of whether monetary policy is 'on course': that is, contracting or expanding demand so as to achieve the desired policy objective(s).

- Monetary policy is pre-emptive. Policy-makers at the Bank of England estimate what the inflation rate is likely to be 18 months to 2 years ahead (the medium term) if policy (that is, interest rates) remains unchanged. If the forecast rate of inflation is too far away from the target rate set by the government, the Bank is prepared to change interest rates immediately to prevent the forecast inflation rate becoming a reality. The Bank is also prepared to raise or lower interest rates to pre-empt or head off any likely adverse effects on the inflation rate of an 'outside shock' hitting the economy. Such a shock can justify a sudden change in interest rates to meet an immediate unforeseen danger.

Supporters claim that the new monetary policy is transparent and accountable, and that the MPC is subject to parliamentary scrutiny. If inflation strays more than 1 percentage point higher or lower than the official target, the 'open letter' system requires that the Governor of the Bank of England write to the Chancellor of the Exchequer, explaining why the divergence has occurred. Any such letter must be published to promote transparency. It is also worth noting that monetary policy (but not fiscal policy) is being used to **manage the level of aggregate demand**, to some extent in the old Keynesian style. However, an independent MPC, unless 'leaned on' by the government, is unlikely to engineer an inflationary pre-election boom as in the old 'political business cycle' of the Keynesian era.

The harmonised index of consumer prices

In June 2003, the government announced its intention to replace the retail price index (RPI) with the **harmonised index of consumer prices (HICP)** used across Europe and in other major economies, including the USA. At the time of the announcement, the RPI (or strictly RPI(X), which measures the underlying rate of inflation) was 3.1%, or about double the 1.6% figure using the HICP measure. The changeover will be accompanied by a reduction in the Bank of England's inflation target, moving it closer to the European Central Bank's 2% inflation ceiling.

Evaluating the success of UK monetary policy

The success of UK monetary policy can be measured by the extent to which the inflation rate target set by the government has been 'hit' since the current framework of monetary policy was created in 1997. Judged in this way, monetary policy has been extremely successful. The rate of inflation measured by RPI(X) has always been between 1% above or below the 2.5% target. However, some commentators believe that this success has been caused in part by luck. A number of factors unrelated to monetary policy have helped to create an environment of low inflation. These include the benign effects of **supply-side policies** implemented in the 1980s and 1990s (*first the pain, and then the gain*) and **globalisation**, which causes import prices to fall and puts downward pressure on domestic cost-push inflation. It remains to be seen whether monetary policy will be as successful in a more turbulent world economy, subject to unexpected hostile outside shocks.

Money and financial markets

Neither Module 2 at AS nor Module 6 at A-level requires a technical understanding of the **nature of money** or of **financial markets**. Nevertheless, it is useful to have a basic understanding of both. A good starting point is the idea of a **portfolio balance decision**, which is illustrated in Figure 10.

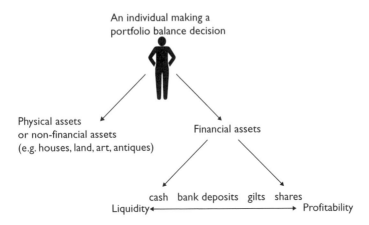

Figure 10 Portfolio balance decisions

Everyone, except the destitute, makes decisions on the form of **asset** in which to keep **wealth**. (An asset is anything that has value.) First, people choose between **physical assets** such as houses (which provide a good **hedge against inflation**) and **financial assets**. Second, they choose the **form of financial asset** to hold. Figure 10 arranges financial assets according to **liquidity** and **profitability**. *Liquidity* measures the ease with which an asset can be converted into money, and the certainty of what it will be worth when converted into money. Providing it is acceptable and can be used as a **means of payment**, money is the most liquid of all assets. But in contrast to less liquid assets such as **shares** and **government bonds** (**gilt-edged securities**, or **gilts**), money earns little or no interest.

Shares and gilts, which are generally more profitable than money, are also **marketable** — they can be sold second hand on the **stock exchange**. The stock exchange is part of the **capital market** on which **public companies (plcs)** sell new issues of shares to raise long-term capital, and on which the government sells new issues of gilts to finance its **budget deficit** (in **fiscal policy**). There are also financial markets in which **short-dated securities** or **bills** (which have a life of a few weeks before they mature) are bought and sold, both as new issues and also second hand. **Treasury bills** are initially sold as new issues by the government, and the markets on which bills are sold are called **money markets**.

Money markets and monetary policy

Banks always need to hold a certain amount of cash to meet possible customer demand, but from the banks' point of view, cash is not profitable. To get round this problem, banks like to hold bills rather than cash to earn *some* profit, knowing that the bills are liquid and can be turned into cash quite easily to meet customers' cash withdrawals. But as a part of monetary policy, the Bank of England deliberately keeps the banks slightly short of cash, knowing that the banks will have to sell bills to the Bank of England, in order to get the cash needed to meet customers' demands. As part of the process of supplying the banks with the cash they need, the Bank of England buys bills and gilts from the banks, at a price which the Bank of England chooses. In this way, the Bank of England sets its **lending rate**, which is the key financial instrument through which monetary policy is currently implemented in the UK.

Examination questions and skills

You should expect two main types of examination question on monetary policy. The first type mentions monetary policy explicitly, asking perhaps for an evaluation of its success, or for a comparison of monetary and fiscal policy. The second type of question is more general, requiring, for example, an evaluation of economic policy in stabilising the business cycle. Monetary policy is not mentioned in the question, but a good answer would explain, analyse and evaluate how monetary policy (and also fiscal policy) might be used to control the level of aggregate demand in the economy. Monetary policy is of course a form of **demand-side policy**. Monetary policy is *not* generally used as a **supply-side policy**, though candidates sometimes wrongly argue that *controlling the money supply* is a supply-side policy.

DRQ2 considers the operation of monetary policy when **deflation** rather than **inflation** poses an economic threat. The first part of EQ1 compares monetary policy and fiscal policy, before asking for an evaluation of recent fiscal policy in the UK. EQ3 asks for an evaluation of the success of recent UK monetary policy.

Common examination errors

- Assuming that modern monetary policy is 'monetarist'.
- Confusing monetary policy with fiscal policy.

- Confusing monetary policy instruments such as the interest rate with the policy objective of controlling inflation.
- Failing to realise that bank deposits are the main form of modern money.
- Failing to link interest rate policy to the central bank's lender of last resort function.
- Failing to understand that interest rate policy may become ineffective as inflation approaches zero (see DRQ2).
- A lack of appreciation of links between monetary policy and the exchange rate.

Fiscal policy, taxation and public expenditure

These notes, which relate to AQA specification section 15.3, prepare you to answer AQA examination questions on:
- the macroeconomic and microeconomic effects of fiscal policy
- interrelationships between fiscal policy and monetary policy
- the structure of taxation and public spending in the UK

Essential information

What you already know about fiscal policy, taxation and public expenditure

When studying AS Module 2 you learnt that **fiscal policy** attempts to achieve the **policy objectives** set by the government using the **fiscal instruments** of **government spending**, **taxation** and the government's **budgetary position** (**balanced budget**, **budget deficit** or **budget surplus**). You also learnt that fiscal policy can be used as a **demand-side policy** or as a **supply-side policy**.

Demand-side fiscal policy

During the Keynesian era, fiscal policy was used primarily to manage the level of aggregate demand in the economy. When **expanding** or **contracting** aggregate demand, fiscal policy brings about a **multiplier effect**.

The government spending multiplier

As Figure 11 illustrates, an increase in government spending (or in any component of aggregate demand) causes **multiple successive changes in national income**, greater in total than the initial increase in government spending. This is the **multiplier**.

To explain the multiplier, we shall assume that there is demand-deficient unemployment, that the levels of taxation and imports are fixed, and that the government is initially balancing its budget (that is, $G = T$). To get rid of demand-deficient unemployment, the Keynesian government decides to run a **budget deficit** by spending an extra £10 billion on road building while keeping taxation unchanged.

- In the first stage of the multiplier process, income of £10 billion is received by building workers who, like everybody in the economy, spend 90p of every pound of income on consumption. (We are therefore assuming that the **marginal propensity to consume (MPC)** is 0.9 throughout the economy.)

- At the second stage of the multiplier process, £9 billion of the £10 billion income is spent on consumer goods and services, with the remaining £1 billion leaking into unspent savings.
- At the third stage, consumer goods sector employees spend £8.1 billion, or 0.9 of the £9 billion received at the second stage of income generation.

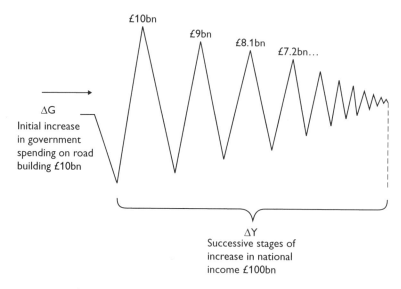

Figure 11 The government spending multiplier

Further stages of income generation then occur, with each successive stage being 0.9 of the previous stage. Each stage is smaller than the preceding stage to the extent that part of income leaks into savings. Assuming that nothing else changes in the time taken for the process to work through the economy, the eventual increase in income (ΔY) resulting from the initial injection of government spending is the sum of all the stages of income generation. ΔY is larger than ΔG, which triggered the initial growth in national income.

The decline of demand-side fiscal policy

Fiscal policy is most powerful for managing aggregate demand when the multiplier is large (for example, 10 in the numerical example in Figure 11). In this situation, expansionary fiscal policy produces an increase in national income much larger than the increase in government spending or tax cut. However, in real life, demand-side fiscal policy is much less powerful. The size of the government spending multiplier is actually quite small (much closer to 1 than to 10) because, at each stage of the multiplier process, a large fraction of income **leaks into imports and taxation as well as into saving**, and is therefore not spent on consumption. Even more significantly, the multiplier process increases *nominal* **national income**, but not necessarily *real*

national income. You must always remember that *nominal* national income can increase in two ways: through **reflation** of **real output**, or through **inflation** of the **price level** (in a **demand-pull inflation**). Keynesians believed that, providing the economy has spare capacity, expansionary fiscal policy stimulates real output more than inflation. But the more fiscal policy was used in this way, the more it injected larger and larger doses of inflation into the UK economy, irrespective of whether the economy was in boom or recession.

Budget deficits, government borrowing and monetary policy

Budget deficits have to be financed by **borrowing** and this **affects monetary policy** in two rather different ways. On the one hand, the government can **borrow short-term from the banking system**. When banks lend to the government, they **create new bank deposits** for the government to spend. **Bank deposits are money**, so this **increases the money supply**. Alternatively, the government can **borrow long-term by selling government bonds** (**gilt-edged securities**, or **gilts**) to pension funds and insurance companies. To persuade these institutions to finance a growing budget deficit, the government may have to **raise interest rates** offered on gilts. But this raises interest rates in general, which discourages private sector investment in capital goods. This is called **crowding out**.

Do not confuse *financing* **a budget deficit** with using higher taxes or reduced public spending to *eliminate* **a budget deficit**. If the latter overshoots, a **budget surplus** results. Budget surpluses allow the government to repay past borrowings, i.e. to reduce the **national debt** (the historically accumulated *stock* **of central government borrowing**).

Supply-side fiscal policy

In the 1980s, demand-side fiscal policy was abandoned and much of fiscal policy became part of **supply-side policy**. Supply-side fiscal policy, which is **micro-economic** rather than **macroeconomic**, tries to alter incentives facing economic agents. Income tax cuts may make people **work harder**, while cuts in the real value of unemployment benefits (compared to disposable income in work) may encourage unskilled and low-paid workers to **choose work rather than unemployment**. Supply-side tax cuts may also encourage **saving**, **investment** and an **entrepreneurial culture**.

The UK government's fiscal rules

The realisation that fiscal policy has a significant effect on monetary policy helps to explain how fiscal policy is used in the UK today. With one exception (noted in the next section), monetary policy rather than fiscal policy is used to manage the level of aggregate demand. By creating conditions in which competitive markets function efficiently, fiscal policy aims instead to achieve macroeconomic stability. The government believes that households and firms must not be hit by nasty unexpected tax increases that affect consumer and business confidence adversely. With this in mind, the government announced a **Code for Fiscal Stability** in 1998, which bases policy on **two fiscal rules**:

- The **golden rule** that over the business cycle the government borrows only to invest in new social capital such as roads and schools, and not to fund current spending, such as welfare benefits. The golden rule means that the government is committed to a budget surplus on *current spending*, but not on *capital spending*.
- The **sustainable investment rule** that public sector debt (mostly central government debt, i.e. the **national debt**) is held at less than 40% of GDP over the business cycle.

The publication of the Code for Fiscal Stability meant that the government recognised officially that fiscal policy should not be used in a **discretionary** way to manage aggregate demand. However, two qualifications must be made. First, a growing budget deficit has led to the government increasing **stealth taxes** (hidden taxes), hoping that the general public will not notice. For electoral reasons, the government is unwilling to increase income tax to reduce the budget deficit, so it has to find other ways of raising revenue. Second, many economists argue that as *nominal* interest rates fall towards zero (which means that when inflation is taken into account, *real* interests may be negative), monetary policy is less and less effective for stimulating aggregate demand — hence the case for using fiscal policy once again as a demand-side policy. This argument is further boosted by the possibility of euro entry. No longer having an independent monetary policy at its disposal, the government would have to use fiscal policy to manage aggregate demand.

Automatic stabilisers

So far we have assumed that the government must choose between demand-side and supply-side fiscal policy. This is not completely true. As the *golden rule* of borrowing indicates, the UK government realises that, while fiscal policy should act predominantly on the supply side of the economy, there is a role for **automatic stabilisers** to influence aggregate demand in the business cycle. Suppose the economy enters recession. As national income falls and unemployment rises, demand-led public spending on unemployment and welfare benefits also rises. But if the income tax system is progressive (see below), the government's tax revenues fall faster than national income. In this way, increased public spending on transfers and declining tax revenues inject demand back into the economy, thereby stabilising and dampening the deflationary impact of the initial fall in aggregate demand, and reducing the overall size of the contractionary multiplier effect.

Automatic stabilisers also operate in the opposite direction to dampen the expansionary effects of an increase in aggregate demand. As incomes and employment rise, the take-up of 'means-tested' welfare benefits and unemployment pay falls automatically, while at the same time tax revenues rise faster than income. Demand is taken out of the economy and the size of the expansionary multiplier is reduced.

Direct and indirect taxation

Income tax is a **direct tax** because the person who receives and benefits from the income is liable to pay the tax. By contrast, most **expenditure taxes** are **indirect taxes**

since the seller of the good, and not the purchaser who benefits from its consumption, is liable to pay the tax. Nevertheless, the purchaser indirectly pays some or all of the tax when the seller passes on the incidence of the tax through a price rise.

Progressive, regressive and proportionate taxation

In a **progressive tax system**, the proportion of a person's income paid in tax increases as income rises, while in a **regressive tax system**, the proportion paid in tax falls. A tax is proportionate if exactly the same proportion of income is paid in tax at all levels of income. Progressiveness can be defined for a single tax or for the tax system as a whole. For income tax to be progressive, the **marginal rate** at which the tax is levied must be higher than the **average rate** — though the average rate, which measures the proportion of income paid in tax, rises as income increases. Conversely, with a regressive income tax, the marginal rate of tax is less than the average rate, while the two are equal in the case of a proportionate tax. As a general rule, the average tax rate indicates the overall **burden** of the tax on the taxpayer, but the marginal rate may affect economic choice and decision making significantly, influencing the choice between work and leisure, and decisions about how much labour to supply.

Progressive taxation cannot by itself redistribute income — a policy of **transfers** in the government's public expenditure programme is required for this. Progressive taxation used on its own merely reduces post-tax income differentials compared to pre-tax differentials. It is often assumed that the UK tax system is highly progressive, being used by governments to reduce inequalities in income and wealth. In fact, wealth taxation (or capital taxation) is almost non-existent in the UK, so inequalities in the distribution of wealth have hardly been affected by the tax system. Many people believe that direct taxes are strongly progressive in the UK, but this is untrue. Direct taxes, which for the most part are income taxes, are only slightly progressive for most income groups, becoming mildly regressive for the richest fifth of households. Overall, the progressiveness of UK income taxes is significantly reduced by the cut in the higher marginal rate of income tax to 40% and by National Insurance contributions that are regressive. And because indirect taxes are mostly regressive, taking a declining proportion of the income of rich households, overall the UK tax system may even be slightly regressive.

Examination questions and skills

Along with monetary policy and supply-side policy (which includes elements of fiscal policy), fiscal policy is one of the most important parts of the Module 6 specification. Some examination questions obviously focus on fiscal policy as a policy *instrument*. Questions on policy *objectives*, such as growth, full employment and price stability, also require knowledge and understanding of fiscal policy and other policy instruments as the means to achieve these objectives. Part (a) of EQ1 asks for an explanation of the difference between fiscal policy and monetary policy, while part (b) requires an evaluation of whether a government committed to the free market should reduce the role of fiscal policy in promoting economic growth.

Common examination errors

- Assuming that fiscal policy always means demand management.
- A lack of awareness of the supply-side elements of modern fiscal policy.
- Failing to understand interrelationships between fiscal policy and monetary policy.
- Defining progressive taxation incorrectly.
- Failing to appreciate the synoptic linkages between fiscal policy in Module 6 and Module 5 topics such as market failures and income distribution.

International trade and globalisation

These notes, which relate to AQA specification section 15.4, prepare you to answer AQA examination questions on:

- comparative advantage, and the case for and against international trade
- the pattern of international trade
- the impact of globalisation on the UK and world economies

Essential information

What you already know about international trade

When studying AS Module 1: Markets and Market Failure, you learnt that **specialisation** and the **division of labour** can increase production possibilities and economic welfare. In Module 2: The National Economy, you learnt that an increase in exports shifts the aggregate demand curve to the right, but that an increase in imports has the opposite effect, taking demand out of the domestic economy.

Widening choice

Imagine a small country such as Iceland in a world without trade. Iceland's **production possibilities** would be limited to the goods and services that its **narrow resource base** enables the country to produce. Likewise, the **consumption possibilities** of Iceland's inhabitants would be restricted to these goods. Iceland's **average costs of production** would also be high because small population size and the absence of export markets mean that **economies of scale** and **long production runs** cannot be achieved.

Compare this with the world of international trade. Imports of raw materials and energy boost Iceland's production possibilities greatly, though in reality, Iceland produces the relatively few goods and services that it is good at producing, and imports all the rest. By exporting goods that it can produce competitively, Iceland benefits from economies of scale and long production runs gained from access to the much larger world market. Likewise, imports of food and other consumer goods present Iceland's inhabitants with a vast array of choice and the possibility of a much higher level of economic welfare and living standards than are possible in a world without trade. To explain these benefits further, we must understand two very important economic principles: the **division of labour**, and **absolute** and **comparative advantage**.

Specialisation and the division of labour

Over 200 years ago, the great classical economist Adam Smith first explained how, within a single firm (a pin factory), output can increase if workers specialise at different manufacturing tasks. Adam Smith believed there are three main reasons why output increases if workers perform specialised tasks. These are:

- there is no need to switch between tasks, so time is saved
- more and better machinery or capital can be employed
- practice makes a worker more efficient or productive at the task he or she is doing

The principle of the division of labour can be extended to explain not only specialisation between separate firms, but also geographical or 'spatial' specialisation, both **internally within a country** and **internationally** between countries.

Absolute advantage and comparative advantage

If a country is best at (or **technically** and **productively efficient** at) producing a good or service, it possesses an **absolute advantage** in the good's production. **Absolute advantage must not be confused with the rather more subtle concept of comparative advantage**.

To explain comparative advantage, we shall pretend that the world economy comprises just two countries, Atlantis and Pacifica, each with just two units of resource (for example, man-years of labour), which can produce only two commodities, guns and butter. Each unit of resource, or indeed a fraction of each unit (because we shall assume that resources or inputs are divisible), can be switched from one industry to another if so desired in each country. Finally, the production possibilities of one unit of resource are:

| In Atlantis: | 4 guns | or | 2 tons of butter |
| In Pacifica: | 1 gun | or | 1 ton of butter |

In terms of technical efficiency, Atlantis is 'best at' — or has an absolute advantage in — producing both guns and butter, but it possesses a comparative advantage only in gun production. This is because **comparative advantage is measured in terms of opportunity cost**, or **what a country gives up when it increases the output of an industry by one unit**. The country that gives up *least* when increasing output of a commodity by one unit possesses the comparative advantage in that good. Ask yourself how many guns Atlantis would have to stop producing or give up in order to increase its butter output by 1 ton. The answer is 2 guns, but Pacifica would only have to give up 1 gun to produce an extra ton of butter. Thus Pacifica possesses a comparative advantage in butter production even though it has an absolute disadvantage in both products.

Output gains from specialisation

Without specialisation, Atlantis and Pacifica produce 5 guns and 3 tons of butter (assuming each country devotes one unit of resource to each industry). If each country specialises in the industry in which it has a comparative advantage, output changes to 8 guns and 2 tons of butter: that is, a *gain* of 3 guns but a *loss* of 1 ton of butter. Although *complete* specialisation produces this result when one country is best at both activities, it is possible to devise a system of *partial* specialisation that results in a net output gain: that is, *more of one good* and *at least as much of the other good*, compared to output withou specialisation. Assume that Pacifica completely specialises, but that Atlantis (the cou try with the absolute advantage in both goods) devotes just enough resource (half a unit) to increase butter production to 3 tons. Atlantis then devotes one and a half units of resource to the production of 6 guns. Total world production is now 6 guns and 3 tons of butter.

As much butter and more guns are produced compared to the earlier 'self-sufficient' situation. Specialisation in accordance with the principle of comparative advantage has therefore increased output.

Import controls or protectionism

Import controls can be divided into **quantity controls** such as **import quotas**, which put a maximum limit on imports, and **tariffs** or **import duties** (and their opposite **export subsidies**), which raise the price of imports (or reduce the price of exports).

Supporters of free trade believe that import controls prevent countries from specialising in activities in which they have a comparative advantage and trading their surpluses. As a result, production takes place inefficiently, and the growth of economic welfare is reduced. But the case for free trade depends to a large extent on some of the assumptions underlying the principle of comparative advantage. Destroy these assumptions and the case for free trade is weakened. One assumption is **constant returns to scale**. In the example above, one unit of resource produces 4 guns or 2 tons of butter in Atlantis whether it is the first unit of resource employed or the millionth unit. But in the real world, **increasing returns to scale** or **decreasing returns to scale** are both possible and indeed likely.

In a world of **increasing returns to scale**, the more a country specialises in a particular industry, the more efficient it becomes, thereby increasing its comparative advantage. On first sight, this increases the case for international specialisation and trade. However, increasing returns to scale can also justify import controls for **developing countries** attempting to promote the growth of new industies. This is the **infant industry** argument. According to this argument, new industries, which in poor countries have not as yet developed increasing returns to scale, need protecting from giant firms in developed countries, where increasing returns to scale have significantly reduced average costs of production. In recent years the infant industry argument has been developed into **strategic trade theory**, which argues that comparative and competitive advantage is often not 'natural' or 'God-given'. Rather, governments can create comparative advantage by nurturing strategically selected industries or economic sectors, typically those that make high-tech goods and use skilled labour. However, the selected sectors must be protected from international competition while they are being built up. The skills that are gained will then spill over to help other sectors in the economy.

When **decreasing returns to scale** occur, specialisation erodes efficiency and destroys any initial comparative advantage. A good example occurs in agriculture when over-specialisation results in monoculture, in which the growing of a single cash crop for export may lead to soil erosion, vulnerability to pests and falling agricultural yields in the future.

Over-specialisation may also cause a country to become particularly vulnerable to sudden changes in demand or to changes in the cost and availability of imported raw materials or energy. Changes in costs, and new inventions and technical progress, can eliminate a country's comparative advantage. The principle of comparative advantage implicitly assumes relatively stable demand and cost conditions. The greater the uncertainty about the future, the weaker is the case for complete special-isation. Indeed, if a country is self-sufficient in all important respects, it is effectively neutralised against the danger of importing recession and unemployment from the rest of the world if international demand collapses.

An argument opposite to the infant industry argument is sometimes made in advanced industrial economies to protect **sunset** or geriatric industries in the older industrial regions from competition from new industries in developing countries. Keynesian economists sometimes advocate the selective use of import controls as a potentially effective **supply-side policy instrument** to prevent unnecessary **deindustrialisation** and to allow orderly rather than disruptive structural change in the manufacturing base of the economy. Some economists also justify import controls to protect an economy from **dumping**, i.e. goods sold below cost to get rid of excess supply in the exporting country.

In addition, as **demerit goods** such as narcotic drugs and weapons and '**bads**' such as pollution clearly indicate, an *output* gain does not necessarily lead to a *welfare* gain. Governments believe that they have a moral duty to ban imports of heroin, cocaine and handguns, to protect the welfare of their citizens. Protection may also be necessary for military and strategic reasons to ensure that a country is relatively self-sufficient in vital foodstuffs, energy and raw materials in time of war.

The pattern of world trade

To many people living in industrial countries during the nineteenth century and the first half of the twentieth century, it must have seemed almost 'natural' that the earliest countries to industrialise, such as Britain, had done so because they possessed a comparative advantage in manufacturing. It probably seemed equally 'natural' that a pattern of world trade should have developed in which industrialised countries in what is now called the **North** exported manufactured goods in exchange for foodstuffs and raw materials produced by countries whose comparative advantage lay in the production of primary products — the countries of the **South**, or developing countries.

The actual pattern of world trade in recent years has changed from the nineteenth-century **North/South exchange** of manufactured goods for primary products. Most of the trade of the developed industrial economies is between themselves and with newly-industrialised countries (NICs); only a relatively small amount is with the rest of the world. World trade is now predominantly **North/North**.

Globalisation

Globalisation is the process **integrating all or most of the world's economies** and making countries increasingly dependent on each other. Globalisation's main features are:

- the **growth of international trade** and the **reduction of trade barriers** — a process encouraged by the **World Trade Organization (WTO)**
- greater **international mobility of capital**
- a significant **increase in the power of international capitalism and multinational corporations (MNCs)**
- a **decrease in governmental power over MNCs**

Free-market economists generally support globalisation and regard it as inevitable. Opponents argue that globalisation is a respectable name for the growing exploitation of the poor, mostly in developing countries, by international capitalism and American economic and cultural imperialism. But globalisation makes no attempt to increase the international mobility of the world's poor, although the highest-paid members of the labour force have become more internationally mobile.

Critics of globalisation use the **dependency theory of trade and development** to argue that developing countries possess little capital because the system of world trade and payments has been organised by developed industrial economies to their own advantage. Export and import prices have, as a general rule, moved in favour of industrialised countries and against primary producers. This means that by exporting the same amount of goods and services to the South, a developed economy can import a greater quantity of raw materials or foodstuffs in exchange. From a developing country's point of view, it must export more in order to buy the same quantity of capital goods or energy, vital for development.

Examination questions and skills

Because the module title is Government Policy, the National and International Economy, at least one of the four questions in each examination is likely to be on international economics. The four main topics to revise in the context of international trade are: the benefits and costs of international trade (particularly in relation to comparative advantage), the case for and against import controls, how the pattern of international trade has changed, and the impact of globalisation on the UK and world economies.

While DRQ1 requires an understanding of the economic factors affecting a range of developed economies, international trade does not figure in this question. By contrast, DRQ4 focuses on the pattern of the UK's international trade and the impact of globalisation on the UK.

Common examination errors

- Writing descriptive accounts of the benefits of free trade devoid of theoretical underpinning analysis.
- Confusing comparative advantage with absolute advantage.
- Failing to appreciate the limitations of the principle of comparative advantage.
- Writing overlong and numerically inaccurate illustrations of comparative advantage.
- Assuming that free trade is advantageous for all countries, all of the time.
- Assuming that countries should always try to maximise exports and minimise imports.
- Asserting without sufficient evidence that globalisation is *always* good or bad.

The balance of payments, exchange rates and EMU

These notes, which relate to AQA specification section 15.4, prepare you to answer AQA examination questions on:
- the difference between the current and capital accounts of the balance of payments
- how the exchange rate is determined in floating and fixed exchange rate systems
- the advantages and disadvantages of European Monetary Union (EMU) and the euro

Essential information

What you already know about the balance of payments, exchange rates and EMU

When studying AS Module 2 you learnt very briefly about the current account of the balance of payments, and about how changes in interest rates (in monetary policy) and the exchange rate can affect the current account. However, Module 2 covered neither the capital account of the balance of payments, nor EMU and the euro.

The current and capital accounts of the balance of payments

The balance of payments measures all the currency flows into and out of an economy within a particular time period, usually a year. Until quite recently, the UK government divided the balance of payments into two main categories:
- the **current account**
- the **capital account**

To fit in with the IMF method of classification, **capital flows**, which comprised the old capital account, now form the **financial account** of the balance of payments, and the term *capital account* is now used to categorise various transfers of income that were previously part of the current account before the new method of classification was adopted. Table 1 shows the current method of classification for 2002.

Table 1 Selected items from the UK balance of payments, 2002 (£m)

The current account *(mostly trade flows)*	
Balance of trade in goods	−35,182
Balance of trade in services	+14,159
Net income flows	+20,646
Net current transfers	−9,247
Balance of payments on current account	**−9,624**
The capital account	
(transfers, which used to be in the current account)	**+1,096**
The financial account	
(capital flows, which used to be in the capital account)	
Net direct investment	+11,128
Net portfolio investment	+61,432
Other capital flows (mostly short-term 'hot money' flows)	−65,831
Drawings on reserves	+459
Financial account balance	**+7,188**
The balance *(errors and omissions)*	**+1,340**

The current account

The **current account** measures the flow of expenditure on goods and services, thus showing the country's income gained and lost from trade. The current account is usually regarded as the most important part of the balance of payments because it reflects the economy's international competitiveness and the extent to which a country is living within its means. Ignoring the other items in the current account, if receipts from exports are less than payments for imports, there is a current account deficit, whereas if receipts exceed payments there is a current account surplus. The current balance is largely determined by adding together the balance of trade in goods and the balance of trade in services. **Trade in goods is sometimes called visible trade, and trade in services is called invisible trade**. As Table 1 shows, the UK has a visible trade deficit and an invisible trade surplus. The earnings of **financial services** in the City of London contribute to the invisible trade surplus. In most years, the invisible surplus is insufficient to offset the visible deficit, so the current account is also in deficit.

The AQA specification **does not** require detailed understanding of all the items in the balance of payments account, but one other item in the current account needs explaining, namely **net income flows**. These provide an important link between the current account and capital flows. British residents (including UK-based multinational companies) invest in capital assets located in other countries. Investment in capital assets is a **capital flow** (see below), but income generated by overseas capital assets is part of the current account. Net income flows are the difference between these inward income flows to UK residents from capital assets owned overseas and outward profit flows to companies such as Toyota, generated by the assets they own in the UK.

Capital flows

Long-term direct capital flows occur when residents of one country invest in productive resources such as factories located abroad. Such investment can be either direct investment (explained in the paragraph above) or portfolio investment. **Portfolio investment** involves the purchase of financial assets rather than physical assets. Table 1 shows that in 2002, more long-term investment flowed into the UK than flowed out. Short-term investment, by contrast, was mainly in the opposite direction. Long-term capital flows are largely a response to comparative advantage, reflecting people's decisions to invest in economic activities and industries located in countries to which comparative advantage has moved. But since changes in comparative advantage usually take place quite slowly, long-term capital flows tend to be relatively stable and predictable. The same is not true of short-term capital flows, which are largely speculative. These flows occur because the owners of funds believe that, by taking advantage of interest rate differences and by gambling on future changes in exchange rates, they can make a quick speculative profit or capital gain by moving funds out of one currency and into another.

Balance of payments equilibrium

Balance of payments equilibrium refers to the **current account** and not to the *whole* of the balance of payments. The current account is in equilibrium when export earnings and inward income flows more or less equal payments for imports and outward income flows. **Disequilibrium** occurs when there is a large deficit or surplus on current account. A large current account deficit may, however, be quite stable — providing it is financed by inward capital flows. As Table 1 shows, this was more or less the situation in the UK in 2002.

Do not confuse *balance of payments equilibrium* with balance of payments *'balance'*. Like any balance sheet, the balance of payments must exactly balance in the sense that all the items included in the balance sheet must sum to zero. The final item in Table 1 explains this. The number in the **balance (errors and omissions)** item is simply the number required to make all the items in the table sum to zero. Note also the small size of the **drawings on reserves** item. This item shows that in 2002 the Bank of England bought pounds by selling reserves of foreign currencies. Central bank intervention in foreign exchange markets by selling or buying reserves is largely determined by whether the exchange rate is floating or fixed. Supporting a fixed exchange rate sometimes requires large-scale selling of reserves, but this is not the case with a freely floating exchange rate. Since 1992, the pound has floated freely; hence the relatively small size of changes in reserves.

Exchange rates

Exchange rates and a foreign exchange market exist because different countries use different currencies to pay for international trade. A currency's exchange rate is simply its external price, expressed in terms of another currency such as the US dollar, or gold, or indeed in terms of an artificial unit such as the **sterling index**, which is the weighted average of a sample of exchange rates of countries with which the UK trades.

Freely floating exchange rates

With **freely floating** (or **cleanly floating**) **exchange rates**, the external value of a country's currency is determined on foreign exchange markets by the forces of demand and supply alone. Figure 12 illustrates how both the exchange rate and the current account of the balance of payments are determined in a freely floating system — subject to the very artificial assumption that there are **no capital flows**. If demand for pounds is D and supply is S_1, the equilibrium exchange rate, expressed against the US dollar, is $1.50. Assuming exports and imports are the only items in the current account of the balance of payments, the current account is also in equilibrium, the value of exports equalling the value of imports at £10 billion, at the equilibrium exchange rate. When there are no capital flows, **exchange rate equilibrium implies balance of payments equilibrium on the current account and vice versa**.

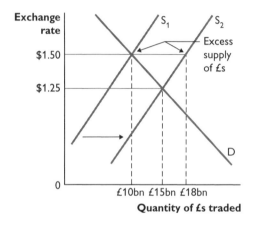

Figure 12 Exchange rate determination on a freely floating exchange rate system

Suppose that some event or 'shock' disturbs this initial equilibrium — for example, an improvement in the quality of foreign-produced goods causing UK residents to increase their demand for imports at all existing sterling prices. Because the demand for foreign exchange to pay for imports increases, the supply curve of pounds shifts rightwards from S_1 to S_2. At the exchange rate of $1.50, the current account is in deficit by £8 billion, which is also the **excess supply of pounds** on the foreign exchange market.

The market mechanism now swings into action to eliminate this excess supply, thereby restoring equilibrium, both for the exchange rate and the current account. Selling of pounds to get rid of excess supply causes the exchange rate to fall, which increases the price competitiveness of British exports and reduces that of imports. The adjustment process continues until a new equilibrium exchange rate is reached at $1.25 to the pound, with exports and imports both equalling £15 billion. Conversely, if the initial equilibrium were disturbed by an event that increased the demand for pounds, the exchange rate would rise to relieve the resulting excess demand for sterling, creating a new equilibrium at a higher exchange rate.

The advantages of floating exchange rates

- When the exchange rate is freely floating, current account surpluses and deficits cease to be a 'policy problem' for governments and a constraint holding back the pursuit of the domestic economic objectives of full employment and growth. The government simply allows market forces to 'look after' the balance of payments, while it concentrates on domestic economic policy. And if, in the pursuit of the domestic objectives of full employment and growth, the inflation rate rises out of line with other countries, the exchange rate falls to restore competitiveness.
- With a floating exchange rate, monetary policy can be completely independent of external conditions and influences. There is no need to keep official reserves to support the exchange rate or to finance a payments deficit. The country's domestic money supply is unaffected by a change in official reserves, and interest rate policy is not determined by the need to protect the exchange rate. The country is free to pursue an 'independent' monetary policy aimed at achieving purely domestic economic objectives, without the need to 'assign' monetary policy and interest rates to support the exchange rate or to attract capital flows into the country to finance a current account deficit.

The disadvantages of freely floating exchange rates

- The argument that a freely floating exchange rate can never be overvalued or undervalued for very long depends crucially on the assumption that speculation and capital flows have no influence on exchange rates. This assumption is wrong. Most foreign exchange deals relate to capital flows and not trade, and exchange rates have become extremely vulnerable to speculative capital or 'hot money' movements. A massive inward capital flow can overvalue an exchange rate and create a serious deficit on the current account.
- Floating exchange rates may unleash a vicious spiral of ever-faster inflation and exchange rate depreciation. Rising import prices caused by a falling exchange rate trigger accelerating domestic inflation, which erodes the export competitiveness won by the initial depreciation of the exchange rate. A further fall in the exchange rate is then required to recover the lost advantage — and so on.

Fixed exchange rates

Figure 13 shows how a government and its central bank maintain a fixed exchange rate. Initially, the government fixes the exchange rate at a central peg of $2.00. Supply and demand determine the day-to-day exchange rate. Providing the exchange rate stays between a ceiling and a floor set when the fixed exchange rate was announced, there is no need for intervention by the central bank and the exchange rate is correctly valued for trade. However, Figure 13 shows the exchange rate falling to the floor of $1.98, possibly because of a speculative capital flow against the currency. At this point the central bank intervenes, raising domestic interest rates to attract capital flows into the currency, and using reserves to support the fixed exchange rate. By selling reserves and buying its own currency, the central bank creates an artificial demand for its own currency.

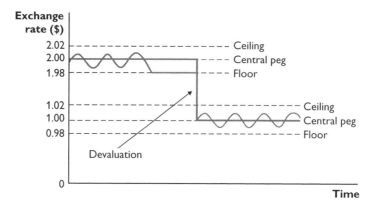

Figure 13 A fixed exchange rate

Persistent support for the currency means that the exchange rate is overvalued, condemning the country to over-priced exports, under-priced imports and a current account deficit. **Devaluation** (or a **lower fixed exchange rate**) is a policy solution — in this case, a devaluation to a new central peg at $1.00. Alternatively, the government could abandon the fixed exchange rate and allow the currency to float and find its own level. This happened in the UK in 1992 on 'Black Wednesday', when the pound dropped out of the **exchange rate mechanism (ERM)** of the EU's **European Monetary System (EMS)**.

European monetary union (EMU) and the euro

The ERM was created to enable the EU to implement common economic policies such as the **common agricultural policy (CAP)** without financial assistance to member countries being distorted by fluctuating exchange rates. But the ERM was a fixed exchange rate system rather than a single currency. The national currencies of member states were always vulnerable to speculative outward capital flows, as happened to the pound in 1992. Partly because of this, the EU decided to go one stage further and replace national currencies with a single currency, the **euro**. As with the ERM, the euro is meant to facilitate much greater **economic union** among the EU's member states.

EU countries currently divide into two groups. Most are in the **Eurozone**, but the UK is among those choosing, at least for the time being, to remain outside the Eurozone and to keep their national currencies. The Eurozone countries are subject to a **common monetary policy** implemented by the **European Central Bank (ECB)** in Frankfurt. The pound's exchange rate floats against the euro, but some other non-Eurozone currencies are more or less fixed against the euro. To learn more about the euro, you must read the candidate's answer to EQ5 and the examiner's comments.

Examination questions and skills

Examination questions are often set on the balance of payments and the exchange rate, and on the linkages between the two. Note also that, although knowledge and understanding of the euro and EMU may be tested in the Unit 4 written paper option (the European Union), the specification for Module 6 has been revised to include European Monetary Union. DRQ4 and EQ5 cover the balance of payments, exchange rates and EMU and the euro.

Common examination errors

- Confusing the current account of the balance of payments with capital flows.
- Failing to appreciate the links between the current account and capital flows.
- Confusing current account equilibrium with balance on the balance of payments.
- Failing to understand how a floating exchange rate may eliminate a current account deficit.
- Writing one-sided polemical essays for or against EMU and the euro.

Questions
&
Answers

This section includes nine examination-style questions designed to be a key learning, revision and exam preparation resource. There are four data-response questions (DRQs) and five essay questions (EQs). The four DRQs are similar in layout, structure and style to the compulsory question in Section A of the Unit 6 examination. Each question can be used as part of a trial or mock exam near the end of your course. Alternatively, as you study a topic in the Content Guidance section of this guide, you could refer selectively to particular sub-parts of each question, as indicated in the 'Examination questions and skills' advice at the end of each topic.

Likewise, you can use the EQs in this section either as timed test questions in the lead-up to the examination or to reinforce your understanding of the specification subject matter, topic by topic, as you proceed through the Content Guidance. The EQs are similar to the three questions, from which you must choose one, in Section B of the Unit 6 examination.

This section also includes:
- A student's answer of grade A–E standard for each DRQ and EQ.
- Examiner's comments on each student's answer explaining — where relevant — how the answer could be improved and a higher grade or mark achieved. These comments are denoted by the symbol 🄴.

Note: It is important to understand the difference between two types of marks that GCE examining boards award for candidates' work: **raw marks** and **uniform standardised marks (USMs)**.

Raw marks are the marks awarded out of 50 (for each DRQ and EQ) by the examiner who reads your script. After all the grade boundaries have been set as raw marks, each candidate's raw mark for the Unit 6 paper is converted into a USM. Uniform standardised marks have the same grade boundaries — for all subjects and all unit exams. These are: grade A: 80%; grade B: 70%; grade C: 60%; grade D: 50%; grade E: 40%.

The marks awarded for students' answers to each DRQ and EQ in the following pages are raw marks and not USMs. A likely grade is indicated at the end of each student's answer, based on the qualities shown in each part of the answer. It must be stressed that the actual raw mark at which a particular grade boundary is set varies from examination to examination, depending on factors such as whether the questions have turned out to be relatively easy or relatively difficult, when compared to questions in previous examinations.

Data-response questions

Question 1

A time of uncertainty for the world economy

Total for this question: 50 marks

Study **Extracts A** and **B**, and answer **all** parts of the question that follows.

Extract A: World economic forecasts

	2000*	% increase per year 2001	2002	2003
Economic growth (GDP)				
USA	5.2	1.9	3.6	3.7
Japan	1.7	0.3	1.4	2.1
UK	3.0	2.5	2.7	2.5
Eurozone	3.4	2.7	3.1	2.5
Inflation				
USA	3.4	3.1	3.6	3.7
Japan	−0.6	−0.1	0.3	0.8
UK	2.1	1.8	2.1	2.2
Eurozone	2.3	2.6	2.0	2.0
Interest rates				
USA	5.8	4.6	4.6	4.7
UK	6.1	5.4	5.4	5.4
Eurozone	4.4	4.5	4.7	4.9

*Actual.

Source: Lloyds TSB *Economic Bulletin*, no. 38, April 2001.

Extract B: Outlook for the world economy

World growth prospects are perhaps more uncertain now than at any time in the last 10 years, notwithstanding the Asian crisis of 1997.

While the growth slowdown was expected by financial markets, its speed and depth have raised fears that the slowdown will end in recession.

We believe there to be three key risks to the global economic outlook worrying 5 the financial markets:

(1) There is growing concern that the European economy will not be able to withstand the effects of the US economic slowdown and the possible Japanese recession, particularly if European interest rates are not cut quickly and deeply.

d ata-response question 1

> **(2)** US consumers will react to falling stock markets by increasing savings and cutting 10
> spending. Falling stock markets will have an adverse effect on world economies.
>
> **(3)** In the USA, households and the company sector have become increasingly
> indebted during the long period of expansion. This now threatens the prospects
> of economic recovery in the USA, and hence the world economy, should the USA
> try to correct these imbalances too quickly. 15
>
> ### The impact of slower US growth
>
> With slower economic growth in Japan, Germany, France and the UK, as a direct result
> of the US slowdown, the risks for the world economy are rising. The impact of the
> US slowdown is larger for the UK economy than for mainland Europe, because the
> UK has a greater trade exposure to the USA and deeper equity market linkages. 20
> But with high consumer and business confidence, a recession is extremely unlikely
> in the UK, unless an outside shock adversely affects either demand conditions or
> supply conditions in the economy.
>
> Source: Lloyds TSB Economic Bulletin, no. 38, April 2001.

(a) Compare the rates of forecast economic growth in the countries shown in
Extract A. (4 marks)

(b) Explain how 'falling stock markets will have an adverse effect on world
economies' (Extract B, line 11). (6 marks)

(c) Analyse how an outside shock might adversely affect either demand conditions
or supply conditions in the economy (Extract B, lines 22–23). (10 marks)

(d) 'In the USA, households and the company sector have become increasingly
indebted during the long period of expansion' (Extract B, lines 12–13). Evaluate
the possible effects of American indebtedness upon both the US economy and
other major world economies. (30 marks)

■ ■ ■

Candidate's answer

(a) Growth was predicted to be positive in all four groups of countries, being highest
in the USA, except in 2001 when US growth might dip below the UK and the
Eurozone, but remain above Japan. None of the countries were predicted to enter
recession (negative growth for two quarters) if the figures are to be believed. It
should be noted that the figures were published in 2001, so all but the first column
are forecasts made before the terrorist attack on the twin towers on 11 September
2001. Most of the figures could therefore be wrong.

> ✍ Good candidates often underachieve on part (a) of a data question because they
> drift away from the question, explaining *causes* of events, when the question asks for
> a *description or a comparison*. This candidate drifts in another way, providing inter-
> esting background material, but unfortunately not making much of a comparison. He

says nothing about Japan, the UK and the Eurozone countries, apart from the fact that growth is positive, and his answer needs a few illustrative statistics.

2/4 marks

(b) Falling stock markets have an adverse effect on economies mainly through their effect on household wealth, and thence on consumption. Consumption is positively related to income and wealth. In America a lot of people own substantial amounts of shares. Bull markets in shares, such as that in the late 1990s, make people feel wealthier. As a result they consume more and save less, partly because their wealth is going up in value. Conversely in a bear market, as happened after April 2000, share prices fall, eroding people's wealth, so they consume less. Recession may occur (as the data indicate in Japan), unless other forms of wealth such as housing continue to rise and offset falling share values. In the UK, fewer people own shares and housing is more significant. However, many people are now beginning to realise that the value of pensions they hope to receive on retirement depends on share prices. Fears of falling pension values may also cause consumption to fall and trigger a possible recession.

🖉 For questions such as this, the mark scheme allows full marks to be earned by one very full explanation, or two or more explanations that are less full. This candidate has followed the first approach and written an excellent answer. Another approach would be to explain the possible effect of falling share prices on businesses. Business confidence (as well as consumer confidence) is adversely affected. Falling share prices also make it more expensive for public limited companies (plcs) to raise new capital through a new share issue, and they make it possible for a hostile takeover raider to acquire victim companies on the cheap.

6/6 marks

(c) Outside shocks are of two types: supply shocks and demand shocks. A Middle East war leading to OPEC suddenly reducing the supply of crude oil and raising its price provides an example of a supply shock. I can analyse the effect of this by using an AD/AS diagram. Before the supply shock, macroeconomic equilibrium is at point X in my diagram, where AD = AS_1. The supply shock raises businesses' costs (via its effect on the cost of energy), and shifts the AS curve upward from AS_1 to AS_2 with a new macro equilibrium at Y. According to the diagram, there are two adverse effects. First, there is a dose of cost-push inflation, with the price level rising from P_1 to P_2. Second, real national output falls from y_1 to y_2, and the economy may now be in recession.

The sudden fall in share prices I referred to in my previous answer is primarily a demand shock, as its main effect may be to induce a sudden unexpected fall in consumer spending in the economy. The question asks for analysis, and the analysis I shall explain is the multiplier theory. According to this theory, a sudden fall in consumer spending (induced by the fall in share prices) triggers multiple and successive stages of decline in national income. When people stop spending, shops receive less income. As a result, they have to sack some of their workers,

ata-response question 1

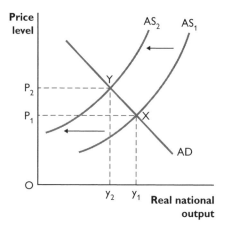

whose income then falls. They in turn spend less, which causes a further fall in income in the economy, and so the process continues.

✑ This question shows how Unit 6 examination questions can be synoptic. The candidate makes use of the AD/AS macroeconomic model and the multiplier concept in his answer. Neither theory is developed beyond the level required in Unit 2 in the AS specification, but this is perfectly adequate for the needs of this particular A2 question. Simple things done well are always preferable to complicated theories messed up.

10/10 marks

(d) Indebtedness basically means the balance of payments deficit on current account. As a generalisation, the current account is in deficit if the monetary value of imports is greater than the monetary value of exports.

A balance of payments deficit on current account can pose a number of problems for a country such as the USA. First, it can mean that the country's industries are uncompetitive. The country's citizens prefer to buy imports from the rest of the world rather than goods and services produced within the country itself. This may be because the country produces bad quality goods, or it may be because the country's exchange rate is overvalued, pricing its goods out of world markets. Both these may pose problems for the country, though the latter may be cured by devaluation or a downward float of the exchange rate. Quality uncompetitiveness is more serious, implying that a deep-seated reorganisation of methods of production might be necessary to make the country's goods and services attractive. Second, a balance of payments deficit is deflationary. It represents a leakage out of the circular flow of income (resulting from the country's citizens preferring to spend on the output of other countries rather than on their own country's production). But for every country suffering a deficit, there must be another country enjoying a surplus (the balance of payments for the whole world must balance). America's deficit therefore promotes an injection of demand into the circular flow of these countries. Such an injection is reflationary (stimulating higher levels of output and employment) if there is spare capacity in the countries that benefit. Alternatively, it is inflationary, pulling up the countries' price levels in a demand-pull inflation, if the other countries have no spare capacity and are close to full employment.

America is, however, in a different position to other countries such as the UK. First, its economy is huge. Internal trade *within* the USA dwarfs its external trade, despite the fact that the latter is very large by world standards. Therefore America's trade deficit only has a very mild deflationary effect on the US economy. This leads to my second point. Because the USA is the only superpower in the world, it can do things that other countries cannot do. Usually when a country has a trade deficit, other countries do not want to hold on to the country's currency that they earn through trade. They sell it and this depresses the country's exchange rate. In the case of the US dollar, this has not been so. Other countries *want* to hold the dollar, despite the US trade deficit. Before 2003, therefore, the US current account deficit transmitted dollars to the rest of the world (when America paid for its imports with its own currency), and these dollars became the world's major source of liquidity. Arguably, the USA was providing a vital service to the rest of the world, reflating the Eurozone and other areas which otherwise might have suffered from demand deficiency and maybe recession. In 2003, however, the USA decided to engineer a fall in the dollar's value against the euro. If this continues, by reducing the current account deficit in the USA, it will boost the American economy. But it will also make Eurozone industries uncompetitive and end or reduce America's export of jobs to Europe.

This is a frustrating answer. The candidate is clearly very knowledgeable, and writes well beyond the demands of A-level. However, his answer is too narrow, addressing only one aspect of indebtedness — a balance of payments deficit on current account. He ignores completely the prompt to discuss and evaluate *household and company sector indebtedness*. These occur when households and companies borrow too much, particularly when interest rates are low. A broader answer, which is necessary to take the score into Levels 4 and 5 (18+ out of 30), needs to discuss and evaluate what might happen to businesses and firms (and thence the US and world economies) following, for example, a rise in interest rates. Investment might crash and firms might be forced into bankruptcy when unable to make interest payments on their debt. Likewise, higher interest rates might cause problems for households. A collapse of investment and/or consumption might trigger a recession in America, which could then spread to the rest of the world. However able you are, in order to do well you must stick to the question. **17/30 marks**

Scored 35/50   70% = grade A

Question 2

Low inflation and the economy

Total for this question: 50 marks

Extract A: Inflation, employment and unemployment in the UK, 1990–2003

	Inflation rate (%) RPI	Inflation rate (%) RPIX	Employment (millions) (ILO count)	Unemployment (millions) (claimant count)	Unemployment (millions) (ILO count)
1990	9.5	8.1	26.83	1.65	1.99
1991	5.9	6.7	26.28	2.27	2.42
1992	3.7	4.7	25.63	2.74	2.79
1993	1.6	3.0	25.28	2.88	2.95
1994	2.4	2.3	25.43	2.60	2.75
1995	3.5	2.9	25.69	2.29	2.47
1996	2.4	3.0	25.94	2.09	2.33
1997	3.1	2.8	26.37	1.58	2.04
1998	3.4	2.6	26.60	1.35	1.77
1999	1.5	2.3	26.90	1.25	1.75
2000	3.0	2.1	27.27	1.09	1.63
2001	1.8	2.1	27.50	0.97	1.43
2002	1.7	2.2	27.66	0.95	1.52
2003	3.0	2.9	27.91	0.95	1.47

Notes:
(i) Changes in the RPI measure the headline rate of inflation, including changes in mortgage interest rates.
(ii) Changes in the RPIX measure the underlying rate of inflation, excluding changes in mortgage interest rates.
(iii) The ILO method of measuring unemployment includes people wanting to work but not claiming benefit.
(iv) 2003 data are for the first two quarters of 2003.

Source: Office for National Statistics website.

Extract B: The low inflation paradise can be hell for borrowers

High inflation is a sign of economic disarray, of a loss of basic values, and a disgrace to the nation, an embarrassment before foreigners. Low inflation is a sign of economic prosperity, social justice and good government. But high inflation is the borrower's friend. In times of high inflation, salaries rise fast and in a short period will more than outweigh debt repayments. Inflation also erodes the capital value of debt. Take a 5 house buyer earning £25,000 a year and borrowing £100,000. If inflation is running at 7.5% a year, the debt will have fallen in 25 years to the equivalent of a debt of £14,000 today.

But low inflation and nominal interest rates may create dangers as damaging as those of high inflation, encouraging consumers to borrow more and save less. Individuals think it is not worth saving today because the low nominal interest rates offered on most savings seem so unattractive.

Meanwhile, consumer debt — four-fifths of it secured on houses — has risen from around 90% of household disposable income in 1989 to more than 120%. Households believe that the time to borrow is when interest rates are low. With unemployment and interest rates at record lows, and house prices still rising, few of us are bothered about how much we owe. Economists call this the problem of money illusion — in this case, households confusing low nominal interest rates with real interest rates. This money illusion distorts rational economic behaviour, making it increasingly difficult for people to pay off their high debts.

When prices don't rise much, high levels of debt make consumers vulnerable to sudden changes in circumstances, for example marriage breakdown, job loss or a hike in interest rates. Regular debt payments look affordable in relation to earnings only as long as earnings continue to rise faster than inflation.

It is even worse during deflation when prices are falling. Then, the value of debt rises against other assets. The dangers of low inflation and deflation are particularly acute for long-term borrowers taking out loans to buy houses. Initially, there is a cash-flow advantage in paying low nominal rates of interest and it is easier to plan ahead, too, because interest payments and returns are not buffeted by swings in inflation. But lower nominal mortgage rates shift the burden of paying the mortgage to the end of the loan.

Money illusion disguises the real cost of debt. Nonetheless, debt secured against housing continues to rise. The government is now worried that consumers, whose attitudes have changed 'from saving to spend to borrowing to spend and pay later', are storing up trouble for themselves. The public needs to save more and borrow less. But stimulating higher saving is not easy. The only way investors can be persuaded to save is by promising high, nominal returns — or by continuing to peddle money illusion and hoodwink savers.

Source: adapted from an article in the *Financial Times*, 14 June 2003.

(a) **Using Extract A, compare the changes that occurred between 1990 and 2003 in the UK's rate of inflation and level of unemployment.** (4 marks)

(b) **Explain two reasons for the changes in unemployment that occurred in the UK between 1990 and 2003.** (6 marks)

(c) **Analyse the view expressed in line 19 of Extract B that 'money illusion distorts rational economic behaviour'.** (10 marks)

(d) **Do you agree that high rates of inflation and interest rates are better for households than deflation and very low interest rates? Justify your answer.** (30 marks)

■ ■ ■

ata-response question 2

Candidate's answer

(a) The data show a generally direct or positive relationship between inflation and unemployment in the UK through the 1990s and early 2000s. Both the headline rate of inflation (measured by changes in the RPI) and the underlying rate of inflation (measured by RPIX) fell through most of the years in the data series. Likewise, after 1993, unemployment also fell according to the UK government's official measures, the claimant count and the ILO method which uses the Labour Force Survey to measure unemployment. However, unemployment increased in the early 1990s, because the UK economy was in recession.

> The candidate shows good understanding but, because no statistics are used to illustrate the points made, the answer earns only half the available marks. Part (a) of a Unit 6 data-response question tests the same lower-order skills as part (a) of a Unit 2 AS data question. However, because this is A-level and not AS, Extract A contains 'background noise' deliberately put there to distract candidates. The candidate did not need to explain the differences between the various data series, or how recession affected unemployment in the early 1990s. **2/4 marks**

(b) Unemployment fell after 1993 as the UK economy came out of recession. Some unemployment was therefore cyclical, caused by deficient aggregate demand. The economy's AD curve shifted rightwards after 1992, causing unemployment to fall. The second reason why unemployment fell relates to supply-side economic policy. This illustrates the saying 'first the pain, and then the gain'. In the 1980s and early 1990s, supply-side policies such as trade union reform and privatisation encouraged employers to get rid of over-manning and to shed redundant labour. This was the 'pain'. But a 'leaner and fitter' UK economy emerged that was more competitive in world markets. New and growing industries based on ICT began to create jobs in the 1990s and unemployment fell. This was the 'gain'.

> The candidate does enough to earn full marks but, like many candidates, he writes rather too glowing an account of the UK economy. Unemployment has indeed fallen, but many of the jobs created are low-wage unskilled 'Mac jobs'. Call centres and other types of service employment provide many of the new jobs, but these jobs may disappear. Service sector employment using ICT and at call centres is beginning to follow manufacturing by moving to low-wage countries. **6/6 marks**

(c) 'Rational economic behaviour' means making decisions a person believes to be in his or her best interest or private interest. When opportunity cost and choice are involved, it means choosing the 'first best' in preference to the 'second best'. People don't, of course, always make the right decisions. They may have undesirable preferences, such as for drugs and other demerit goods that will eventually harm them. Many choices involve conflict between short-term and long-term private benefit maximisation — for example, the choice between studying for an exam and going out and having a good time! Imperfect information also means that people often lack sufficient information to make best interest decisions.

'Money illusion', which results from imperfect information, occurs when people confuse nominal values with the real values, falsely believing that the real value is the same as the nominal value. As Extract B indicates, inflation, and indeed deflation, cause money illusion. I shall provide two examples. A firm offers its workers a pay rise of 2% when inflation is 3%. Money illusion occurs if the workers wrongly believe their real pay has increased, when in fact it has fallen by 1%. My second example is pertinent to Extract B, illustrating the effect of low inflation rates on the real rate of interest. Suppose the Bank of England cuts its lending rate (a nominal rate) to 3% when inflation edges up to 3.5%. If commercial banks follow the Bank of England, the real rate of interest offered to savers is negative, –0.5%. The real value of savings falls, and it is not worth saving. However, people will continue to save, partly because they haven't realised that real interest rates are negative.

✓ This is an excellent answer, easily reaching Level 3 (8–10 marks). My only criticism is that, by expanding on his explanation of rational economic behaviour in the first paragraph, the candidate's own opportunity cost may be insufficient time to complete the exam paper. **10/10 marks**

(d) This question is primarily about the benefits and costs of inflation compared with the benefits and costs of deflation. Lines 1–3 of Extract B state that 'high inflation is a sign of economic disarray, of a loss of basic values, and a disgrace to the nation, an embarrassment before foreigners', while 'low inflation is a sign of economic prosperity, social justice and good government'. The extract then argues that this is not necessarily the case. I shall develop this argument in my answer. Provided the rate of inflation is relatively low and *stable*, and therefore easy to *anticipate*, the benefits of inflation may exceed the costs. In this situation, by boosting consumer and business confidence, inflation lubricates the economy and makes it run more smoothly. Inflation also generally means 'today is a better time to buy goods than tomorrow'. Because people bring forward consumption decisions to avoid tomorrow's higher prices, the economy is less likely to suffer from deficient aggregate demand and the paradox of thrift. (For individuals, thrift or saving is a virtuous activity. But if everybody saves — and if firms are unwilling to borrow the savings to finance spending on capital goods — deficient aggregate demand emerges, which may trigger a recession.)

Suppose the government decides to eliminate inflation and establish absolutely stable prices. If the government uses contractionary monetary or fiscal policies to achieve this aim, there is a danger it may 'kill the goose that laid the golden egg'. Contracting demand destroys consumer and business confidence, and it can trigger the adverse consequences of the paradox of thrift. Governments should therefore be prepared to live with low and stable inflation — though they must also be prepared to contract aggregate demand to head off a sudden increase in inflation that would otherwise destabilise rather than lubricate the economy.

There are three reasons why deflation is dangerous. First, tomorrow is better than today for buying goods, when prices are falling. Why buy an expensive car

today, if tomorrow it will be cheaper? But when tomorrow comes, consumption should be further delayed because it becomes cheaper again on the following day. In other words, despite negative real interest rates, for consumer durables, people may stop spending when prices are falling.

Second, deflation occurs in recessions, though since the Second World War, *disinflation* (or a slowdown in the rate of inflation) rather than *literal* deflation (falling prices) has generally occurred in recessions. In recessions, incomes are low and workers fear for their jobs. Deflation therefore accompanies and exacerbates depressed business and consumer confidence.

The third reason for fearing deflation relates to the conditions in the UK housing market that are mentioned in Extract B. In times of rapid inflation, owner occupiers who are already on the 'housing ladder' do very well, particularly when the rate of house price inflation exceeds the rate of general inflation. Inflation erodes the real value of the mortgage taken out at the time of house purchase. But when inflation slows down — particularly house price inflation — this is no longer the case. A mortgage, which seems very cheap (because both nominal and real interest rates are low) at the time of house purchase, becomes much more expensive in real terms in later years, because low inflation only reduces the real value of the stock of debt by a small amount. House purchasers who fail to appreciate this fact may borrow too much. If the economy enters recession and the mortgagee loses his job, or if a collapse in house prices produces the problem of negative equity (debt or borrowings exceeding assets), owner occupiers may be unable to repay their debts.

In conclusion, rapidly accelerating inflation — rising possibly into a hyper-inflation that destroys normal economic activity — is obviously bad. However, deflation can also be bad, largely because deflation is associated with recession and economic stagnation. The best outcome is therefore a low and stable rate of inflation. When the rate of inflation is stable, it is relatively easy to anticipate. Economic agents build the inflation rate into consumption and investment decisions without suffering adverse distorting effects. In this situation, the benefits of inflation exceed the costs. We must all be prepared to live with at least some inflation and to resist calls for absolute price stability or deflation.

This is generally a very good answer that resists the temptation to write a shopping list of the benefits and costs of inflation. The answer contains enough analysis and evaluation to reach Level 4 (18–24 marks), but because the answer is a little too narrow, it does not quite reach Level 5. The question asks whether high rates of inflation and interest rates are better for households than deflation and very low interest rates. The candidate provides a good and interesting discussion and evaluation of the question in terms of inflation, but there is not enough in his answer about the effects of high and low interest rates (nominal and real). Greater balance between the effects of high and low inflation and high and low interest rates is required for the answer to reach Level 5. **24/30 marks**

Scored 42/50 84% = grade A

Question 3

Exchange rates, the dollar and the Eurozone

Total for this question: 50 marks

Extract A: Up and down: changes in exchange rates, 2001–03

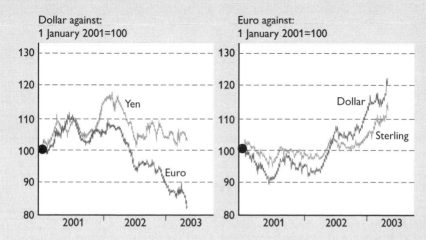

Source: *The Economist*, 12 May 2003.

Extract B: USA declares war on the euro

In the second half of the 1990s, the US economy expanded by some 4% per year in real terms. But in 2001 and 2002, when the dollar was strong and the euro weak, the US average growth rate fell to 1.3%. In an effort to boost economic growth, the US government tried to talk the economy up, but it did not work. The Americans are now trying another tactic: a rapid devaluation of the dollar against the rest of the world in general, and the Eurozone in particular.

While the euro was weak, Eurozone companies such as Mercedes and Renault did very well, whether they were exporting or competing in domestic markets with foreign companies. But the dollar's fall of 14% in 2002 against a weighted average of other major currencies has made Eurozone economies uncompetitive. The fact that the exchange rates of many Asian countries, including China, are fixed against the dollar, has made this worse. It means that the Eurozone bears the brunt of the dollar devaluation, and that the euro is losing competitiveness with Asian tiger economies as well as with the USA.

5

10

data-response question 3

> The rise in the euro and the fall of the dollar have brought squeals of pain from 15
> French and German exporters at a time when the German economy is in recession
> and the French economy perilously close. The world's industrial economies are awash
> with excess capacity, most are experiencing disinflation, and some are threatened
> by outright deflation. The Americans have encouraged the dollar to fall because
> they are frustrated with the demand-management policies, or lack of them, in Europe. 20
> Coordinated expansion by the Eurozone countries to counter the global slowdown
> would help the USA as well as European countries. A healthy global economy needs
> multiple engines of growth. European Union countries must expand demand, and they
> must also introduce structural reforms or supply-side policies. On the demand side,
> the Eurozone's Stability and Growth Pact constrains the use of fiscal policy to expand 25
> demand, while the European Central Bank (ECB) seems still to be obsessed with
> fighting the last inflationary war. On the supply side, Eurozone governments are
> reluctant to overcome political opposition and the hostility of trade unions to introduce
> the necessary labour market reforms.
>
> Source: adapted from an article in the *Observer*, 25 May 2003.

(a) **Using Extract A, compare the changes in exchange rates that occurred between 2001 and 2003.** (4 marks)

(b) **Line 4 of Extract B states that 'the US government tried to talk the economy up'. Explain how 'talking up' the economy may boost economic growth.** (6 marks)

(c) **Lines 11–12 of Extract B state that 'the exchange rates of many Asian countries, including China, are fixed against the dollar'. Analyse how the decision by Asian governments to fix exchange rates against the US dollar may affect the UK economy.** (10 marks)

(d) **Evaluate the view expressed in lines 23–24 of Extract B that European Union countries must expand demand, and that they must also introduce structural reforms or supply-side policies.** (30 marks)

■ ■ ■

Candidate's answer

(a) Extract A shows the dollar and the euro having exactly the same exchange rate at the beginning of 2001. One dollar exchanged for one euro, since both exchange rates were 100. Over the next two years, the dollar's exchange rate fell against the euro, while the euro rose against the dollar.

> ✏ There are two reasons why this is a poor answer. First, the candidate does not understand index numbers. The fact that 100 provides the base year index for both currencies in January 2001, does not mean that one dollar exchanged for one euro. Second, he makes no mention of the yen or sterling and no comparison of the differences between the early and later parts of the period. Note also that if the first part of the second sentence is true, the second part does not need stating. When the dollar falls against the euro, the euro must rise against the dollar. **1/4 marks**

(b) Governments wish to 'talk up' the economy as part of a successful public relations campaign. In recent years, we have all got used to political 'spin'. Spin tries to cast every news event in the best possible light for the government. Governments have learnt the art of being economical with the truth. They have become very good at conning the general public.

This answer contains no relevant economics and so earns no marks. It seems that the candidate has studied government and politics and is trying to apply political concepts to an economics question. However, information brought in from other subjects must develop, rather than replace, the economics of the answer.

'Talking up' an economy may boost consumer and business confidence, thereby shifting the AS curve rightward. For this to be effective, however, the government policies must be credible, i.e. people must have confidence in the government and in its ability to manage the economy.   **0/6 marks**

(c) Since the collapse of communism, the USA has been the world's only superpower and the dollar is the world's super-currency. As the extracts show, until quite recently the dollar's exchange rate rose against the rest of the world. The governments of a number of poorer countries fixed their currencies against the dollar, possibly to gain some of the strength of the dollar. South American countries such as Argentina did this because their own currencies were very weak, and the dollar was increasingly used by businesses and citizens within their own countries. This wasn't really true for Asian countries such as China, but these countries were big exporters to America. Fixing their currencies against the dollar meant that the prices of their goods in America were stable.

Countries in southeast Asia are primary producers, producing commodities such as rubber and teak which they export to America and to other industrial countries. As long as the dollar's exchange rate rose against the euro and the pound, these exports became more expensive in Europe, but not in America. However, the recent fall in the dollar has produced the opposite effect, reducing the export price of goods produced in countries whose exchange rates are fixed against the dollar. Because rubber and teak cannot be produced in the UK and have to be imported, the main effect on the UK economy is to increase our demand for these imports, and possibly to reduce cost-push inflationary pressure.

The explanation of how falling exchange rates in Asian countries may affect the UK via their effect on the prices of imported raw materials just takes the answer to Level 2 (4–7 marks). Even here, though, the explanation is incomplete. The candidate could earn extra marks by explaining how exchange rates affect import prices, and how lower import prices reduce cost-push inflation in the UK. However, the relatively poor grade is more the result of the lack of any mention or explanation of the fact that Asian countries, and increasingly China, export manufactured goods to the UK. Via their link to the dollar, falling Asian exchange rates contribute not only to reduced inflation in the UK, but also to the collapse of British manufacturing industries.   **4/10 marks**

data-response question 3

(d) I agree that Eurozone countries such as France and Germany must introduce structural reforms or supply-side policies. However, I don't agree that they should manage the level of aggregate demand. The latter only leads to inflation, which is a bad thing.

Britain and America successfully introduced supply-side policies in the 1980s and 1990s. These policies were necessary to correct the mistakes of decades of Keynesian mismanagement of the economy. The Keynesians had relied on managing demand, believing that the government can 'spend its way out of a recession'. But, in the UK at least, expanding aggregate demand sent the economy into 'slumpflation' or 'stagflation' of excessive demand-pull inflation accompanied by rising unemployment.

Fortunately, the supply-side policies introduced by Mrs Thatcher's governments in the 1980s corrected all this. At the microeconomic level, the Thatcher governments introduced policies of economic liberalisation, namely privatisation, marketisation (or commercialisation) and deregulation. President Ronald Reagan also liberalised the American economy. Supply-side policies became associated with Thatcherism in the UK, and with Reaganomics in the USA. At the macroeconomic level, Mrs Thatcher's governments cut taxes and reduced welfare benefits relative to rates of pay in work. The supply-side policies successfully increased incentives to work, to be entrepreneurial, to save and to invest, with an *enabling* culture replacing the previous *dependency* culture. Meanwhile, by reducing 'crowding out', the tax cuts freed resources previously used by the *wealth-consuming* public sector for the *wealth-creating* private sector to use more productively and efficiently.

In other countries in the European Union, things were very different. Believing that they had a greater social obligation to their populations, governments refused to privatise state-owned industries such as Air France, or to reduce the very generous level at which welfare benefits were set. As a result, supply-side reforms similar to those introduced in the UK were rejected. Tax rates remained high, and too many workers preferred to remain unemployed, living off benefits, than to take a low-paid job.

The lack of supply-side reform in continental Europe has led some economists to identify an economic 'disease', called eurosclerosis. In human form, sclerosis hardens the bones and makes old people vulnerable to breaking arms and legs when they fall over. Eurosclerosis hardens the European economies, rendering them unable to change to meet competition from more flexible, lower-waged economies such as the Asian tiger economies. Eurosclerosis, which results from a lack of appropriate supply-side policies, has undoubtedly contributed to the current relatively poor economic performance of the Eurozone economies. They are suffering from sluggish rates of economic growth, which in some cases are falling into recession, and from much higher rates of unemployment than in the UK. So, for the reasons I have just explained, I believe that the Eurozone countries must introduce structural reforms or supply-side policies, but I don't see demand-side policies as being appropriate.

After writing disappointing answers to the first three parts of the question, the candidate writes a stronger answer to the evaluative section. Overall, and perhaps slightly generously, the answer reaches a high Level 3 (10–17 marks). Because the answer concentrates on supply-side problems and policy, with little *accurate* mention of the role of aggregate demand, it cannot reach Level 4.

Like many students, the candidate seems to believe that under *all* circumstances, supply-side policies and demand-side policies are incompatible with each other, and that supply-side policies should always be chosen in preference to the management of aggregate demand. This view, which stems from the experience of the Keynesian era when policy-makers ignored both the need for supply-side reform and the adverse effects of relying too much on demand management, is simply wrong. Recent British governments, Labour and Conservative, have managed aggregate demand very successfully, though the task has been delegated to monetary policy and the Bank of England.

The candidate should have argued that there is a role for demand management, but to be successful, the government might first have to put in place appropriate supply-side reforms to make the economy efficient, competitive and flexible. Such policies shift the economy's LRAS curve rightwards, *enabling* the country to produce more output. But *potential* output can be produced only if there is enough demand to absorb the extra output.

The candidate could also argue that demand management policies might have to be used to counter the adverse effects on the economy of an outside shock hitting and destabilising the economy. Extract B mentions that the Eurozone's Stability and Growth Pact constrains the use of fiscal policy to expand demand. A very good answer may have picked up on this point to argue how, because of the pact, Eurozone governments lack the freedom to use fiscal policy to manage demand. With regard to monetary policy, the European Central Bank has also been accused of being too deflationary and of being obsessed with 'fighting the last inflationary war'. The Eurozone may be using monetary policy as well as fiscal policy in the wrong way.   **17/30 marks**

Scored 22/50   44% = grade D

Question 4
World trade and globalisation

Total for this question: 50 marks

Extract A: The changing pattern of the UK's international trade

	1955		1992		2000	
UK trade with:	Exports (%)	Imports (%)	Exports (%)	Imports (%)	Exports (%)	Imports (%)
EU	15.0	12.6	56.4	52.5	57.3	51.0
Other west European countries	13.9	13.1	7.9	11.6	4.0	6.0
North America	12.0	19.5	13.0	12.6	18.0	15.4
Other developed countries	21.1	14.2	3.6	7.1	5.8	8.3
Oil-exporting developing countries	5.1	9.2	5.6	2.5	3.3	2.0
Rest of the world	32.9	31.4	13.5	13.7	11.6	17.3

Source: *Annual Abstract of Statistics*, various (ONS).

Extract B: Globalisation

Modern globalisation has been made possible primarily by improvements in information and communication technology (ICT), as well as by developments in more traditional forms of technology. Examples of globalisation include service industries in the UK dealing with customers through call centres in India and a sportswear manufacturer designing its products in Europe, making them in southeast Asia and   5
finally selling them in North America. However, sceptics argue that globalisation is nothing more than part of a process that has been going on for many centuries and that the current international economy is in many ways less open and integrated than it was in the period leading up to the First World War.

Protesters believe that by replacing domestic economic life with an economy that   10
is heavily influenced or controlled from overseas, globalisation surrenders power in developing economies to First World based multinational corporations (MNCs). For some of its critics, low-paid sweatshop workers, GM seed pressed on developing world farmers, selling off state-owned industry to qualify for IMF and World Bank loans and the increasing dominance of US and European corporate culture across the globe   15
have come to symbolise globalisation.

But not everyone agrees that globalisation is necessarily evil. Some economists say that globalisation has not worked because there has not been enough of it. If all countries get rid of all protectionist measures, the 'invisible hand' of the market will promote international trade and benefit poor countries as well as rich ones.   20

Source: adapted from articles in the *Guardian*, 31 October 2002.

Extract C: History debunks the free trade myth

Imagine you are visiting a developing country. It has the highest average tariff rate in the world. It is doing everything against the advice of the IMF, the World Bank, the WTO and the international investment community.

Sounds like a recipe for development disaster? But no. The country is the USA — only that the time is around 1880, when its income level was similar to that of   5
Indonesia today. Despite wrong policies and sub-standard institutions, it was then one of the fastest-growing — and rapidly becoming one of the richest — countries in the world, especially in relation to trade policy. Many top economists, including Adam Smith, had been telling Americans for over a century that they should not protect their industries — exactly what today's development orthodoxy tells developing   10
countries.

But the Americans knew exactly what the game was. Many knew all too clearly that Britain, which was preaching free trade to their country, became rich on the basis of protectionism and subsidies. The fact is that rich countries did not develop on the basis of the policies and institutions they now recommend to developing countries.   15
Virtually all of them used tariff protection and subsidies to develop their industries. In the earlier stages of their development, they did not even have basic institutions such as democracy, a central bank and a professional civil service.

Once they became rich, these countries started demanding that the poorer countries practise free trade and introduce 'advanced' institutions — if necessary   20
through colonialism and unequal treaties. Friedrich List, the leading German economist of the mid-19th century, argued that in this way the more developed countries wanted to 'kick away the ladder' with which they climbed to the top and so deny poorer countries the chance to develop.

'Kicking the ladder' has been resumed with renewed vigour in the last two   25
decades, when developed countries have exerted enormous pressures on developing countries to adopt free trade, deregulate their economies, open their capital markets, and adopt 'best-practice' institutions such as strong patent laws. But there is no 'best-practice' policy that everyone should use. The WTO rules should be rewritten so that the developing countries can use tariffs and subsidies more actively for industrial   30
development.

Source: adapted from an article in the *Guardian*, 24 June 2002.

(a) **Using Extract A, describe the changes that occurred in the pattern of the UK's international trade between 1955 and 2000.** (4 marks)

(b) **Explain one advantage and one disadvantage of globalisation increasing the power of multinational corporations in developing economies.** (6 marks)

(c) **Analyse how international trade may benefit all countries.** (10 marks)

(d) **In the light of the information in the data, evaluate the case for a poor country using import controls to protect itself from the adverse effects of globalisation forced on it by richer countries.** (30 marks)

data-response question 4

Candidate's answer

(a) Extract A shows that over the 45-year period from 1955 to 2000, the UK's pattern of international trade changed from being largely 'North/South' to becoming 'North/North'. The UK now trades mainly with other developed countries (i.e. the countries of the 'North'), and especially with the European Union countries. In 1955, only 15% of UK exports and 12.6% of UK imports were with the EU (though the EU did not exist at the time). By contrast, 26.2% of UK exports and 23.4% of UK imports related to developing countries. By 2000, this situation was reversed: respectively 57.3% and 51.0% of UK exports and imports were with EU countries, while exports and imports relating to developing countries had fallen to 9.1% for exports and 10.3% for imports. As a word of caution, it is not clear whether the trade figures for 1955 relate to the six original EU members, or the 15 countries in the EU in 2000.

> This is an excellent answer that earns all **4 marks**, despite the lack of reference to the intermediate year (1992) shown in the data. The answer displays exactly the right balance of overview and illustration with a *few appropriate* statistics selected from the table.   **4/4 marks**

(b) Extract B identifies low-paid sweat-shop workers as a disadvantage for developing countries, resulting from the activities of an MNC. Multinational corporations locate factories in developing countries to employ cheap labour in order to cut production costs.

But the reverse argument may also hold true. Supporters of multinational corporations argue that MNCs introduce 'best practice' First World methods of production, which improve pay and working conditions for local labour compared to that on offer from indigenous or locally based firms.

> The candidate has *stated* an advantage and a disadvantage, but he needs to explain the statements. Some elaboration is required as to *why* First World based MNCs may exploit local workers and/or improve local pay and working conditions.   **4/6 marks**

(c) International trade may benefit *all* countries, primarily through increased output and welfare made possible by specialising in accordance with the principle of comparative advantage. Comparative advantage is measured by the other products a country gives up producing when devoting scarce resources to the production of a particular good or service. Comparative advantage is defined by *opportunity* cost. Because resources are scarce, the production of one good means a country has to reduce production of other goods (assuming full employment with the country on its production possibility frontier). The country which gives up producing *least* other goods when producing a particular good, possesses the comparative advantage in that good. If all countries specialise in the goods in which they possess a comparative advantage and then trade their surpluses with each other, the world's production possibility frontier shifts outward. When consumed, the extra output increases human happiness.

> 🖉 As this is a 10-mark rather than a 30-mark question, the candidate wisely restricts his answer to analysis of a single issue, comparative advantage. He explains the concept very clearly without introducing a numerical example. Numerical examples take time to construct (and have their own opportunity cost), and it is very easy to make errors that render the example meaningless. The quality and relevance of the candidate's analysis are sufficient to make this a Level 3 (8–10 mark) answer. However, the candidate achieves a low rather than a high Level 3 score. To earn more marks, some reference must be made to the 'all' in the question.   **8/10 marks**

(d) The economist Paul Krugman identifies three different views of international trade, which he calls *classical*, *strategic* and *mercantilist*. My answer to part (c) was based on the classical view that all countries can benefit from higher output and economic welfare, providing they specialise in accordance with the principle of comparative advantage.

Classical trade theory assumes that comparative advantage is 'god-given' and beyond human control. Strategic trade theory disputes this view, arguing that, protected by strategically-chosen import controls, a country can create comparative and competitive advantage for its industries.

But governments may pretend to be *strategic*, when really they are *mercantilist*. Believing that 'exports are good and imports are bad', a mercantilist government tries to use all possible means to maximise its trade surplus at the expense of other countries. If free trade can achieve this aim, the government pressurises other countries to drop import controls. But if its own industries become un-competitive and go into decline, the government switches tack and uses all available arguments ('unfair' competition, dumping and strategic trade theory) to justify the introduction of import controls. The author of Extract C obviously believes that developed countries are mercantilist. He argues that rich countries, having benefited from protectionism while they established their wealth, are now putting pressure on poor countries to abandon import controls and to allow multi-national corporations unlimited access to their economies. Some argue that free trade theory is used to justify First World economic imperialism.

I shall now use economic welfare theory to show how a country (though not *all* countries) can benefit from setting an *optimal* tariff. The left-hand panel of my diagram below illustrates a standard argument *against* import controls. In the absence of tariffs, the country imports goods at the world price P_w. When a tariff is imposed, the good's price rises to P_{w+t}, and consumer surplus falls by the area D + A + B + C. But not all of the fall is a loss to the *whole* economy. Areas D and B are transferred respectively to domestic firms (as producer surplus) and to the government (as tariff revenue). Taking account of these transfers, the economy's net welfare loss caused by the tariff is A + C.

data-response question 4

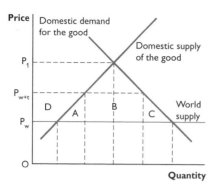
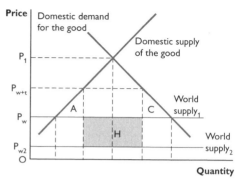

But an optimal tariff (shown in the right-hand panel of the diagram) produces a net *welfare gain* for the country concerned (though not for the countries exporting the goods). This is because the tariff reduces demand for the good to such an extent that the good's world price falls to P_{w2}. The net welfare gain enjoyed by the importing country is shown by the area H – (A + C). Area H, which is the extra tariff revenue resulting from increasing the tariff to match the fall in the good's world price, more than offsets the net loss of consumer welfare (A + C).

Arguably, rich countries such as the USA possess sufficient economic power to benefit from optimal tariffs. Poor developing countries lack this power. They may, however, use another argument, the theory of the 'second best', to justify import controls. The 'second-best' argument stems from the fact that the 'first best', free trade in a world of fully employed economies and perfect markets, is unattainable. Therefore a poor country can settle legitimately for the 'second best'. Employing resources inefficiently, protected by tariffs, is better than not employing resources at all.

🖉 This is an excellent answer displaying a knowledge of economic theory that extends beyond the demands of the A-level specification. The candidate loses a couple of marks by failing to provide evaluation at the end of the answer, although some evaluation marks are earned on a point-by-point basis as the answer develops.

28/30 marks

Scored 44/50   88% = grade A

Essay questions

Question 1
Monetary and fiscal policy

(a) **Distinguish between monetary and fiscal policy and explain how both can be used to manage aggregate demand.** (20 marks)

(b) **Evaluate the fiscal policy that might be implemented by a free-market orientated government.** (30 marks)

■ ■ ■

Candidate's answer

(a) Monetary policy is part of macroeconomic policy through which the government tries to achieve its objectives, by using monetary instruments such as controls on bank lending and the raising or lowering of interest rates. Likewise, fiscal policy is the part of government policy which uses fiscal instruments (altering the structure and rates of taxation, public spending and the public sector's budgetary position) to achieve the government's policy objectives.

Fiscal policy and monetary policy may be assigned to different policy objectives; alternatively they may be used to support each other or even to achieve the same objective, such as the management of aggregate demand. In the Keynesian era, fiscal policy was indeed associated primarily with the management of aggregate demand. However, since the Keynesian era ended in the 1970s, free-market-inspired governments have generally rejected the use of taxation and public spending as discretionary instruments of demand management. They argue that when fiscal policy is used to stimulate or reflate aggregate demand in order to achieve growth and full employment, the policy will be at best ineffective, and at worst damaging. Any growth of output and employment will be short-lived, and in the long term the main effect is to accelerate inflation, thereby destroying the conditions necessary for satisfactory market performance and 'wealth creation'.

Both fiscal policy and monetary policy manage aggregate demand by shifting the aggregate demand (AD) curve rightward or leftward. The diagram (overleaf) shows a rightward shift of aggregate demand which increases real output from y_1 to y_2, and increases the price level in a demand-pull inflation from P_1 to P_2. Extra spending injected into the economy increases people's income. At the next stage, people spend a fraction of their increased income on consumption, which creates more income for other people. Multiple and successive stages of income generation follow, each smaller than the previous stage because a fraction of income received is held back and not spent.

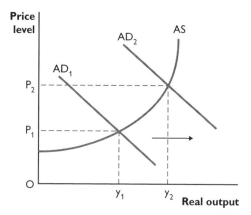

There is a danger of answering this question much too narrowly, namely by defining monetary policy solely in terms of 'monetarism' and fiscal policy in terms of 'Keynesian demand management'. Fortunately, this candidate does not do this. She writes a good answer, but nevertheless does not earn full marks. She asserts that fiscal and monetary policy both shift the AD curve, but she needs to explain this. For example, she should explain how, in monetary policy, an interest rate cut stimulates consumption and investment. The question is synoptic, testing candidates' knowledge of the components of aggregate demand in Module 2: The National Economy.   **14/20 marks**

(b) A free-market-orientated government would probably subordinate fiscal policy to the needs of monetary policy. Free-market economists believe that control of public spending and public sector borrowing (in the government's fiscal policy) is a necessary precondition for responsible control of the monetary conditions (in monetary policy). Instead of using fiscal policy to manage demand, a free-market-orientated government might base policy on a medium-term fiscal 'rule' to reduce public spending, taxation and government borrowing as proportions of national output. Besides reducing the inflationary effects of 'big government spending', such a fiscal policy should prevent public spending from 'crowding out' the private sector. Free-market economists believe that public sector spending and borrowing 'crowd out' the private sector in two ways. 'Resource crowding out' occurs when the government uses resources in its public spending programme, which might otherwise have been employed in private sector production. Second, 'financial crowding out' occurs when the government borrows to finance public sector spending. An increase in government borrowing causes interest rates to rise, which increases the cost of investment finance for the private sector.

As well as adopting a fiscal policy which is consistent with the monetary policy aim of controlling inflation, free-market economists recommend that the macroeconomic elements of fiscal policy should be subordinated to a more microeconomic fiscal policy based on tax cuts to create incentives to work, save and be entrepreneurial. They argue that workers respond to cuts in income tax rates by working harder. Conversely, high rates of income tax and a high overall tax burden create disincentives which, by reducing national income as taxation increases, also reduce the government's total tax revenue.

Free-market economists argue that the increase in the tax burden in the Keynesian era, which was required to finance a growing government sector, raised the average tax rate towards or beyond the critical point at which tax revenue is maximised. In this situation, any further tax increases would have the perverse effect of reducing the government's total tax revenue still further. Indeed, tax cuts rather than tax increases may raise total tax revenue, since a growing national output, stimulated by lower tax rates, will yield higher total revenue despite the reduced tax rates. The effect is reinforced by a decline in tax evasion and avoidance as these activities become less worthwhile at less penal tax rates.

Given that governments have to levy taxes to raise revenue to finance necessary government expenditure, free-market economists believe that the structure or pattern of taxation should be switched away from taxes on income and capital and towards taxation of expenditure. All taxes are of course unpopular and disliked and resisted to some extent by taxpayers, but some are more unpopular than others. Free-market economists believe that expenditure taxes are less unpopular than income tax, and therefore more acceptable to taxpayers. Although initially disliked when first imposed or when tax rates are raised, expenditure taxes are less 'visible' than income taxes. Taxpayers soon get used to expenditure taxes and learn to live with them. Free-market economists also argue that expenditure taxes have a further significant advantage. Unlike income taxes, expenditure taxes do not have a substitution effect, which distorts the choice between labour and leisure — a distortion which supply-siders believe operates against the supply of labour and in favour of not working. Indeed, in so far as expenditure taxes — like all taxes — introduce some distortion into the economic system, they do so by raising the price of consumer goods, which encourages households to substitute saving in place of consumption. This is an important virtue in the free-market view of the world.

🖉 Candidates sometimes argue that because free-market economists generally reject the use of fiscal policy to manage the level of aggregate demand, this means that they do not recommend any use of fiscal policy. The candidate clearly rejects this erroneous line of approach and writes an excellent Level 5 answer (25–30 marks), detailing a range of possible ways in which free-market economists might use fiscal policy. **29/30 marks**

Scored 43/50   86% = grade A

Question 2
Economic growth and economic welfare

(a) Explain the meaning of economic growth, and the factors that cause it.   (20 marks)

(b) Do you agree that growing national income inevitably increases economic welfare? Justify your answer.   (30 marks)

■ ■ ■

Candidate's answer

(a) There are two ways of defining economic growth, relating respectively to the short run and to the long run. In the short run, economic growth takes place by moving from a point inside the country's production possibility frontier to a point on or closer to the frontier. This happens when there are unemployed resources in the economy. Defined in this way, economic growth simply takes up the slack in the economy. Short-run economic growth, which is better defined as economic *recovery*, is shown by the movement from point A to point B on the production possibility diagram drawn below.

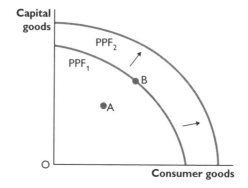

Long-run economic growth (or *true* growth) is defined as an increase in the economy's production potential. It is depicted by an outward movement in the economy's production possibility frontier from PPF$_1$ to PPF$_2$. Whether it is defined in terms of the short run or the long run, economic growth must not be confused with economic *development*. Development relates to the improvement in the general well-being of the whole population, whereas growth is much more narrowly defined. My answer to part (b) of the question will return to this distinction.

If I could explain fully the various factors that cause economic growth, I might win the Nobel prize in economics! Economists can certainly identify factors that *contribute* to economic growth, but they are unable to explain with complete certainty why growth happens in some countries but not in others. There is general agreement that investment is an important factor, but investment on its own, at least in physical rather than human capital, is not enough. Investment enlarges a country's stock of machines and other capital goods, but these are of little use unless the country's infrastructure and labour force are appropriate. One reason why Asian tiger economies such as South Korea have grown much faster than African countries relates to the labour force. Cheap labour is obviously attractive, as China's current very fast growth illustrates, but many countries have cheap, and usually uneducated, labour, but don't unfortunately enjoy high growth rates. Likewise, a rich resource base of industrial raw materials and energy can obviously help, but some of the most rapid recent economic growth has taken place in countries with no minerals or energy, and whose main economic resource is an educated and trained population. In Asia, in particular, investment in education and training seems to have been the most significant cause of growth. Education and training have equipped the tiger economies with highly productive labour forces, but African countries have not achieved this result.

However, I still don't think I have yet identified the single most important cause of growth, which is very difficult to create by economic factors alone. I am referring to the country's cultural system and legal structure. A country must have an entrepreneurial spirit among its citizens and a legal system that encourages the establishment and the on-going growth of successful local businesses. Inward investment by overseas-based multinational corporations can also be an important factor, bringing in capital and best practice, but this must be additional to, and not a replacement for, the growth of indigenous businesses within the country. Rapid technical progress is an important factor for the growth of the world economy, though a poor country can generally import technical progress from abroad. Some forms of progress, such as developments in ICT, have turned low-waged countries into much more attractive locations for investment. The movement of call centres from the UK to India provides a very recent example. The emergence of appropriate financial intermediaries and a capital market are important. These institutions channel savings (both local savings if there are any, and funds raised abroad) into productive investment. Likewise, the law of contract is very important for encouraging trust and the growth of voluntary commercial transactions. Without an appropriate legal system and an enforced law of contract, 'gangster capitalism' may emerge, which leads not to proper economic growth, but to crime, speculation and unjustifiable inequalities that hinder the growth process.

🖉 This is an extremely good answer, but it does not quite earn full marks. Though it is especially strong on overview, surveying and prioritising the main causes of growth, it is a little thin on how factors such as investment lead to economic growth. Perhaps fewer points are needed, but more detail. **18/20 marks**

(b) In my answer to part (a), I referred to the fact that economic growth must not be confused with economic development. Economic *development* improves economic welfare or human happiness. By contrast, economic growth creates the conditions in which welfare can improve. By this I mean that economic growth *facilitates* improvements in economic welfare, but does not itself bring these about. If, for example, a businessman becomes extremely rich, his personal economic welfare will almost certainly have increased. But if he has made himself rich by cutting the wages of his labour force and by polluting the land and other aspects of the environment in which his workers live, his personal gain may be more than matched by the welfare loss he forces on others. Economic growth has occurred, but not economic development. Economic development measures many more factors affecting the quality of human existence than growing real GDP. The factors include the quality of the environment, people's health, vulnerability to disease and sanitation, the availability of good education, and the extent to which the distributions of income and wealth are reasonably fair or equitable.

An obvious example of economic growth not increasing economic welfare occurs when population grows faster than real GDP. In this situation, real income per head of population falls, and most of the people end up consuming fewer material goods and services.

Economic growth produces resource depletion (the result of using up finite resources) and resource degradation (for example, pollution), both of which can adversely affect economic welfare. Rich countries may, of course, grow success-fully and dump dirty industrial processes and pollution on poor countries that are only too glad to have some source of employment. At least in the short run, therefore, economic welfare can increase among the rich, without the beneficiaries having to pay for the true cost of their activities. However, pollution and resource depletion do not respect national boundaries. In the long run, the rich as well as the poor will be affected adversely, experiencing, for example, the malevolent effects of climatic change brought about by global warming.

On the basis of my arguments, I shall conclude that economic growth, providing it promotes economic development, can increase the economic welfare of the broad mass of people, but it is certainly not *inevitable* that growth produces this result. It is more likely to do so if growth is *sustainable*. This involves using renewable rather than finite resources, and abolishing or at least minimising the effect of growth on resource degradation. To finish my essay on a slightly optimistic note, as people get richer they demand more normal goods. For most people, an attractive environment and a sense of other people's well-being are both normal goods. In the richer liberal democracies of the world, people vote for governments that promise to make growth more sustainable. Unfortunately, however, people are also short-sighted, tending to prefer immediate self-gratification to policies which, although they would increase economic welfare throughout the world, would also have the short-term effect of making voters poorer.

This is an excellent answer, strong on analysis and evaluation, that easily reaches Level 5 (25–30 marks). As with his answer to part (a), the candidate is especially strong on overview, though once again he can be criticised for not giving very much detail on the particular arguments he makes. However, in examination conditions, it is impossible to do everything. The candidate's confident and well-organised overview more than makes up for any deficiencies of detail.   **28/30 marks**

Scored 46/50   92% = grade A

Question 3

Inflation

(a) 'Inflation is initially caused by excess demand, but sustained by increasing
   costs of production.' Explain this statement. (20 marks)
(b) Evaluate the view that the Bank of England's monetary policy has been
   solely responsible for reducing inflation and allowing the economy to expand. (30 marks)

■ ■ ■

Candidate's answer

(a) Inflation, which can be defined as a continuous or persistent rise in the average price level, can be caused by excess demand and by rising production costs. These are called demand-pull and cost-push causes of inflation. There are two main theories of demand-pull inflation, the monetarist and the Keynesian theories.

The monetarist theory, which is based on the quantity theory of money, assumes that people wish to hold money solely to spend on goods and services, and that they don't hold idle or passive money which is not spent. If the money supply or stock of money in the economy increases at a faster rate than real output, people spend their excess money balances and the price level is pulled up.

By contrast, the Keynesian demand-pull theory locates the underlying cause or engine of inflation in factors other than money. To get elected, governments have to deliver public services. High levels of government spending, when added to household consumer spending and to investment spending by businesses, are the main source of excess demand in the economy.

However, many Keynesians favour cost-push rather than demand-pull theories of inflation. When unemployment falls, labour shortages increase and make unions more powerful. Business costs increase and trigger cost-push inflation. Pay relativities and different rates of productivity growth are responsible for important aspects of cost-push inflation. To illustrate this, I shall assume two 'productivity sectors' in the economy, one with a high rate of growth of labour productivity (for example, 6% a year) and the other with a 0% rate. Firms in the 'high-productivity' sector may be willing to grant money wage increases of 6%, though they would resist paying wage increases higher than 6%. Providing wage increases do not exceed 6%, cost inflation does not occur in this sector. But suppose workers in the 'zero-productivity' sector bargain with their employers to maintain comparability or to restore differentials relative to less skilled workers employed in the other sector, i.e. they aim for the same percentage wage increase as workers achieved in the 'high-productivity' sector. If a 6% wage increase is granted to *all* workers, cost inflation will be generated as firms in the 'zero-productivity' sector pass on the increased wage costs to consumers as price increases.

The inflationary process then continues through a wage–price 'spiral' and 'leapfrogging'. A wage–price 'spiral' occurs when workers in both sectors realise that real wage increases have been eroded by price inflation. This unleashes further money wage increases, which temporarily restore the real wage increases — until a further bout of price inflation erodes the real wage once again. 'Leapfrogging' occurs when pay rises lead to retaliation by other workers attempting to restore or improve on their original position in the pecking order or pay league table.

📝 Had the
uestion been 'compare the theories of demand-pull and cost-push inflation', this would have been a very good answer. But to do well, candidates must adapt their knowledge to the needs of the question. The question could be answered by explaining that inflation, initially caused by excess demand, triggers the cost-push inflationary process, which the candidate explains very well. The cost-push process continues even when there is little or no excess demand, probably reinforced by the way in which continuing inflation affects expectations. If workers believe inflation will continue, they behave in an inflationary way because they fear they will lose out unless their own wages increase. This is the effect of the psychology of inflation. But because the candidate has written two separate accounts of the causes of inflation, her total mark is restricted. **13/20 marks**

(b) The key to my answer to this question lies in the word 'solely'. There is little doubt that the monetary policy implemented by the Monetary Policy Committee (MPC) of the Bank of England has contributed to reducing inflation and allowing the economy to expand, but it has not been the *sole* factor responsible for this success. Before I survey and assess the relative significance of the other factors that have played a role, I shall first explain and evaluate the role of monetary policy.

I think there are five main reasons why UK monetary policy has been successful in controlling inflation without forcing the economy into recession. My reasons relate to the Bank of England's model of how the economy works, the expertise of the MPC, the improved quality of information available to the MPC, the fact that monetary policy is pre-emptive, all of which lead to the fifth reason, the policy's credibility.

(1) Unless governments or central banks are very lucky, the success of policy decisions depends on the quality of the macroeconomic model used to explain how the economy works, and for forecasting purposes. The Bank of England uses a highly sophisticated econometric model of the economy, which is regularly updated in the light of new information.

(2) Before the Bank of England was made operationally independent in 1997, the general public's trust of monetary policy was often reduced by the suspicion that policy was being manipulated for political reasons, especially before elections. The fact that monetary policy is now implemented by non-political experts has arguably increased the credibility of the policy.

(3) The Bank of England has a much higher quality of statistical information than used to be the case, about the current and recent performance of the economy and of other economies, such as the USA and the Eurozone economies, that might affect UK performance.

(4) UK monetary policy is pre-emptive. This means that the Bank is prepared to take action quickly (by raising or cutting interest rates) if its economic model or a sudden outside shock indicates either that inflation will accelerate or that the economy may enter recession at some point in the medium-term future.

(5) Successful pre-emption, along with the general public's confidence in the experts implementing the policy, makes the policy credible. Credibility means that the general public behave in ways that are consistent with the policy's objectives, which in turn helps the policy to be successful.

The factors I have just surveyed have all contributed to the recent success of monetary policy. The Bank of England has been prepared to raise interest rates to head off or pre-empt an increase in inflation, but equally, it has been willing to cut interest rates to stop consumption and investment falling and starting a recession. However, monetary policy would not have been successful if the general state of the national and world economies had not favoured low inflation and an expanding economy. Because I am running out of time, I can only mention other relevant factors very briefly. First, the supply-side policies implemented in the 1980s and 1990s have turned the UK into a much more competitive and flexible economy, capable of adjusting quickly to new circumstances. Second, the combined effects of globalisation, the pound's relatively high exchange rate and the falling prices of commodities such as copper and coffee beans have all tended to reduce inflation in the UK. In conclusion, it is relatively easy to implement monetary policy success-fully when conditions are benign in the national and world economies. Monetary policy will be much more sorely tested if the national or global economies are suddenly hit by unexpected demand-side or supply-side shocks.

In contrast to her answer to part (a), where she avoided the main issue posed by the question, for part (b) the candidate focuses her answer strictly on the question. The answer reaches Level 5 (25–30 marks). To earn full marks, the candidate needs to develop a few of the points she has made. For example, she might summarise the Bank of England's view of how the economy works. Writing just a little too much on part (a) means she has too little time to survey the factors other than monetary policy responsible for low inflation and a growing economy. It is also worth noting that, in October 2003, great doubt was thrown on the accuracy of many of the economic statistics published by the Office for National Statistics (ONS). This may negate the candidate's assertion about the high quality of the statistical information used by the Bank of England. **26/30 marks**

Scored 39/50   78% = grade A

Question 4
Unemployment

(a) **Carefully explain the meaning of the natural rate of unemployment.** (20 marks)

(b) **Evaluate the view that reducing the natural rate of unemployment is better for the economy than reducing unemployment below its natural rate.** (30 marks)

■ ■ ■

Candidate's answer

(a) Monetarists and other free-market economists use the term 'the natural level of employment' to describe the level of employment at which the labour market clears — at the real wage rate at which the aggregate demand for labour equals the aggregate supply of labour. They argue that there is no involuntary unemployment when unemployment is at its natural level. However, there will be *some* voluntary frictional unemployment: the natural level of unemployment. (The natural *rate* of unemployment (NRU) is the natural *level* of unemployment calculated as a percentage of the labour force.)

The natural rate of unemployment can also be explained in terms of the long-run Phillips curve. In 1968, Milton Friedman introduced the theory of the expectations-augmented Phillips curve when he argued that a stable relationship between inflation and unemployment, as depicted by the original Phillips curve, had never existed. According to Friedman, the apparent relationship identified by Phillips was at best short term and unstable. Friedman's theory suggests that the only 'true' long-term relationship between unemployment and inflation lies along a vertical line, on which trade-offs are not possible, running through the natural rate of unemployment. This is the long-run Phillips curve (LRPC).

The relationship between the LRPC and the economy's aggregate labour market is shown in the diagram opposite. The economy's natural level of *employment* is determined in the upper panel of the diagram at the market-clearing real wage at which the aggregate demand for labour equals the aggregate supply of labour. The natural level of *unemployment* is then calculated by subtracting the natural level of employment from the total labour force. The diagram has been drawn so that the natural level of *unemployment* is depicted immediately below the natural level of *employment* in the upper panel. If either or both of the aggregate demand for, and aggregate supply of, labour curves shift rightwards in the upper panel, the natural level of employment will increase. Simultaneously, the LRPC and the natural level of unemployment will shift leftwards in the lower panel.

The natural rate of unemployment or NRU is sometimes called the non-accelerating inflation rate of unemployment (NAIRU). However, the NRU and the NAIRU are similar but not quite identical concepts. The NRU is derived from the free-market theory of the aggregate labour market, which assumes that market

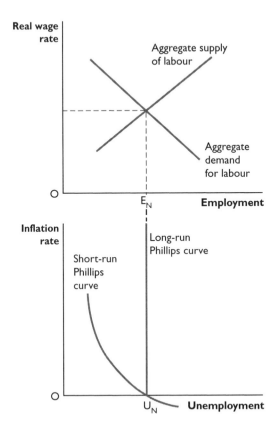

forces quickly get rid of any unemployment other than voluntary frictional unemployment. By contrast, the NAIRU derives from new-Keynesian theory. For new-Keynesians, the NAIRU contains an element of structural unemployment, caused by rigidities in labour markets, as well as the frictional unemployment which accounts for the NRU.

☑ This answer earns full marks. The candidate understands the NRU fully and she has drawn excellent diagrams.   **20/20 marks**

(b) Free-market economists have sometimes argued that it is irresponsible to use Keynesian demand management policies to try to reduce unemployment below its natural rate. They argue that any (temporary) reduction of unemployment below its natural rate cannot be sustained. They believe that when demand expands to reduce unemployment below its natural rate, inflation always accelerates, and that accelerating inflation destroys the conditions in which a high level of employment can be maintained.

Most free-market economists want to reduce unemployment (though some argue that some unemployment is necessary to 'discipline' the workforce). They believe the correct way to reduce unemployment is to reduce the natural rate itself. Supply-side policies should be used for this purpose. But unlike the Keynesians, who in the past have recommended interventionist supply-side policies which increase the role of the government, free-market supply-side policy reduces the role of the state in the economy. Appropriate policies (for a free-market economist) include tax and public expenditure cuts to reduce the burden of taxation on the private sector and to create incentives to individuals and firms, and all micro-economic policies which might make individual markets more competitive, efficient and adaptable to change. Reductions in unemployment benefits are sometimes recommended, to reduce their value relative to take-home pay in a low-paid job.

Because free-market economists believe that it is irresponsible to expand demand to reduce unemployment below its natural rate, it is sometimes said that they reject demand expansion completely. For the most part, this is untrue, though some free marketeers, the new-classical economists, believe that as output and employment are always at or very near their natural levels and rates, expansionary fiscal and monetary policy should only be used with very great caution. However, many free-market economists agree with the Keynesians that as long as unemploy-ment is significantly *above* its natural rate (and output *below* its natural level), there is a role for demand expansion, primarily through lower interest rates and monetary policy. This will close the economy's output gap — the gap between actual output and the level of output that would occur had the economy been growing continuously at its trend rate of growth. They accept that temporary demand-deficient unemployment, in the form of cyclical unemployment, can exist in the recessionary phase of the business cycle, and that a demand stimulus is the appropriate response.

This is a very good answer which contains a significant amount of accurate analysis and thoughtful evaluation. Quite rightly, the candidate accepts that virtually all economists, except extreme free-marketeers, now agree that demand management policies should be used to stabilise the business cycle and to make sure that there is sufficient demand to absorb extra output produced by successful supply-side policies. The fact that most economists once again accept a role for demand management means that there is now an area of consensus and synthesis which unites rather than separates a large part of the economics profession.

28/30 marks

Scored 48/50   96% = grade A

Question 5

Exchange rates and the euro

(a) Explain the effect of a fall in the exchange rate upon a country's balance of
   payments on current account. (20 marks)

(b) Assess the view that the economic conditions are now right for the UK to
   replace the pound with the euro. (30 marks)

■ ■ ■

Candidate's answer

(a) As the pair of graphs below shows, the effect of a fall in the exchange rate upon a country's balance of payments depends to a large extent on domestic elasticity of demand for imports and overseas elasticity of demand for the country's exports. A fall in the exchange rate (that is, a devaluation, depreciation or downward float) raises the price of imports from P_1 to P_2, and reduces the price of exports from P_3 to P_4. The higher price of imports means that UK residents reduce spending by the area (B), but increase spending by (A) because the goods they still import are now more expensive. By contrast, cheaper exports cause overseas residents to increase spending by the area (D), but their spending also falls by (C) because each unit of exports now earns less foreign currency. If domestic demand for imports and overseas demand for the country's exports are both elastic (that is, greater than 1), then (B + D) > (A + C), so the current account improves. However, if both elasticities are highly inelastic, a fall in the exchange rate perversely worsens the current account.

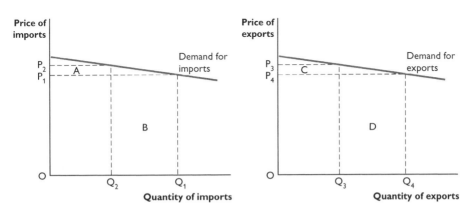

Matters are, however, complicated by the 'J-curve' effect shown in my second diagram. This shows the current account worsening immediately after the fall in the exchange rate, before it improves. This is explained by the fact that, immediately after the devaluation, the demand curves for imports and exports are likely to be inelastic. (The time period in question affects elasticities, and short-run elasticities are much more inelastic than long-run elasticities.)

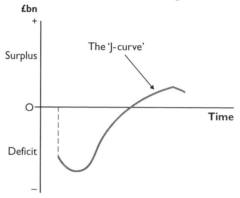

Finally, elasticity of supply is also relevant. For the current account to improve following a devaluation, demand must switch away from overseas-produced goods to domestically produced substitutes. This requires plenty of spare capacity in the domestic economy, which is capable of producing goods that are quality-competitive as well as price-competitive. If this capacity does not exist, the supply of domestically produced output is inelastic and the economy cannot produce the extra output to meet the switching of demand. In this situation, the fall in the exchange rate produces demand-pull inflation (as well as the cost-push inflation induced by higher import prices), which quickly wipes out the improved price competitiveness won by the devaluation.

🖉 This is an extremely good answer that easily earns full marks. Note how the candidate's answer is synoptic in the excellent way in which the Module 1 concept of elasticity is applied. **20/20 marks**

(b) When considering whether the economic conditions are now right for the pound to be replaced by the euro, I shall consider the UK government's five economic tests. Undoubtedly, the two main tests are convergence and flexibility as these can affect the other tests, namely investment, employment and the financial sector. So far, only the test on compatibility with the City (the financial sector test) has been completely passed — at least according to the UK government.

Complete convergence is impossible prior to entry. It is highly unlikely that Britain, with its greater ties with North America and other non-EU countries, will ever fully converge with Eurozone members, even if it eventually joins. Convergence is necessary so that the UK's business cycle can be synchronised with those of Eurozone countries. When the ECB raises or lowers interest rates to manage aggregate demand within the Eurozone, it is important that the UK is at the same point in the business cycle as core Eurozone countries such as Germany and France. For example, if the UK is booming when Germany is in recession, the

ECB will be under pressure to cut interest rates to help Germany. But this would overheat the UK economy and exacerbate a problem related to the UK housing market. Owner-occupancy is greater in the UK than in most Eurozone countries, and UK house buyers have variable interest rate mortgages in contrast to the fixed interest rates common in the Eurozone. A cut in interest rates therefore has little effect on continental housing markets but a great effect in the UK. It would unleash a spending spree among UK owner-occupiers suddenly benefiting from a fall in mortgage interest repayments.

If monetary policy is to be taken away from the Bank of England, as euro entry dictates, the UK must be able to switch back to using fiscal policy to manage demand. Currently, however, the deflationary bias of the EU's Stability and Growth Pact limits the freedom of Eurozone members to use fiscal policy to head off a deep recession. But with recession and unemployment now rampant in the Eurozone, the pact fights yesterday's problem of inflation instead of the current problem of stagnation and possible deflation. The pact means there is little a national government can do to get out of recession. The time can only be right for Britain to join the euro if the Stability and Growth Pact is abandoned.

In terms of employment, supply-side policies adopted in the UK but not in mainland Europe mean that Britain has a more flexible labour market — measured in terms of the ease of hiring and firing workers. However, British workers are more poorly trained than continental workers and their language skills are much worse. Geographical mobility of labour is poor both within the UK and across EU frontiers. However, this and similar problems such as the poor quality of British management are intractable and not subject to quick policy fixes. They will remain problems whether or not Britain joins the euro.

Employment and investment will both be greatly affected by the exchange rate if and when the pound disappears. Currently the pound is floating. In the event of overvaluation, the exchange rate can fall to restore competitiveness, unless of course, as has been the case in the recent past, a hot money inflow makes the pound continuously overvalued. If Britain joins the euro, devaluation is no longer possible. Entry at an overvalued level would probably burden the UK with permanent trading uncompetitiveness and deflation. Joining at the right exchange rate is essential if Britain is to benefit from the euro. Fortunately, the pound's exchange rate has been falling recently, and conditions have become more suited to Britain joining the euro.

Conditions are now better than they have been for euro entry, though not perfect. Ultimately, however, it is a *political* as well as an *economic* decision, and here, by committing itself to a referendum in which the electorate is almost certain to vote 'no', the British government is boxed in.

This is a very good Level 5 answer (25–30 marks) to a question that might catch a lot of candidates out. It is easy to misinterpret this question as *Evaluate the case for and against joining the euro*. But this is not the question. The question assumes that a case can be made for joining the euro, and asks about whether the conditions for

essay question 5

successful entry are in place. Of course, it is possible to challenge the question by arguing that, in *any* circumstance, euro entry is bad for the UK, so therefore conditions can *never* be right for entry. Nevertheless, to earn a high mark, such an answer would still need to consider arguments related to the exchange rate, monetary and fiscal policy, etc. This particular question illustrates how, over the years, subtle changes take place in topical questions. By the time you read this question and the candidate's answer, it may be out of date. Think carefully about how the agenda has moved on and the likely stance of a really up-to-date question on the UK and the EU. Returning to the question, despite writing a very good answer, the candidate does not earn full marks. He has not *quite* covered all of the UK government's five tests for euro entry, which he mentioned at the beginning of his answer.   **27/30 marks**

Scored 47/50   94% = grade A